Better Management and Effective Leadership through the Indian Scriptures

Better Management and Effective Leadership through the Indian Scriptures

Narayanji Misra

Pustak Mahal®, Delhi

J-3/16 , Daryaganj, New Delhi-110002

☎ 23276539, 23272783, 23272784 • *Fax:* 011-23260518

E-mail: info@pustakmahal.com • *Website:* www.pustakmahal.com

London Office

51, Severn Crescents, Slough, Berkshire, SL 38 UU, England

E-mail: pustakmahaluk@pustakmahal.com

Sales Centre

10-B, Netaji Subhash Marg, Daryaganj, New Delhi-110002

☎ 23268292, 23268293, 23279900 • *Fax:* 011-23280567

Branch Offices

Bangalore: ☎ 22234025

E-mail: pmblr@sancharnet.in • pustak@sancharnet.in

Mumbai: ☎ 22010941

E-mail: rapidex@bom5.vsnl.net.in

Patna: ☎ 3094193 • *Telefax:* 0612-2302719

E-mail: rapidexptn@rediffmail.com

Hyderabad: *Telefax:* 040-24737290

E-mail: pustakmahalhyd@yahoo.co.in

ISBN 978-81-223-0996-6

Edition : 2008

Printed at : Param Offsetters, Okhla, New Delhi-110020

I dedicate this book to my wife
Smt Prakash Misra
who has really been a
lighthouse
(Prakash Stambh)
in my life
and
to all my children and also
to my readers,
with my best wishes.

Dr. Karan Singh
MEMBER OF PARLIAMENT
(RAJYA SABHA)

3, NYAYA MARG
CHANAKYAPURI
NEW DELHI - 110 021

FOREWORD

Contrary to the popular belief that Indian scriptures deal exclusively with philosophy, the fact is that they cover the whole gamut of human activities including politics, phonetics, economics, grammar, metallurgy, medicine, astronomy and many more. Each of these areas needs management and leadership, and Narayanji Misra has made an interesting attempt to excerpt from our scriptural heritage the teachings specifically for the manager/leader.

The author has arranged his material under various chapters as 'The Basic Managerial Functions', 'Cultivate Your Workforce', 'Manager as a Leader', 'Managing by Least Supervision', 'The Knack of Winning People', 'Crisis Management', 'Manage Your Speaking', 'Manage Your Writing', 'Discipline', 'Money Management' and so on. Each of these areas is of perennial interest to managers today, and a careful study of aphorisms contained in this book will certainly be an illuminating exercise. I am sure Misra's work will be of much interest not only to students of Management but to the general public as well.

Karan Singh

KARAN SINGH

Tel. : 2611-1744, 2611-5291 Fax : 2687-3171
E-mail : karansingh@karansingh.com

The First, rather, the Last Words

I have been in the field of personnel management almost all my life. In order to improve my working capacities and to gain excellence, I have gone through a number of works written by various western scholars like Robert Owen, Peter F. Druker, F.W. Taylor and others. Just four or five years back, my uncle (Late) Shri Anand Swarupji Misra, who has a number of scholarly works to his credit, such as *Nana Saheb Peshwa*, *Jawahar Lal Nehru*, *Kannauj Ka Itihas*, *Shri Harsh and his Naishad Charit*, *Judicial Propriety* and others, advised me that I should also go through ancient Indian scriptures and creative writings like Valmiki's *Ramayana* and Vedavyas' *Mahabharata*. Thereafter, I started reading the Vedas, Upanishads and also the works of Manu,*Œukra* and Kautilya who have codified rules to be followed in day-to-day life and also in the moments of deep distress or periods of crises.

My uncle also advised me to take to serious writing and compile a book on the matter I had gathered. He told me that I am in the seventeenth place in the tradition of the great Sanskrit poet Shri Harsh who wrote classical works like *Naishad Charit*, *Khandan Khand Khadya*, and many others. He said if I take to writing, I shall find my forefathers guiding me. I, then, took to writing most of which has already been published. After my retirement in 1988, I was invited by a number of institutions to deliver lectures on 'Personnel Management'. In these lectures, I tried to say what western scholars have written on this subject. But then I thought as to why I should not add to it the expert knowledge which is contained in the Indian scriptures. Thereafter I decided to arrange the material gathered from Indian sources scientifically and subject-wise and write it down. Thus this book, *Towards Management Excellence* (the name of this book proposed by the author), came to life.

I hereby acknowledge that this is a very humble attempt and sincerely hope that this work will inspire more of the erudite scholars to go through the works of Indian sages, thinkers and philosophers, and write better and more meaningful books. I also hope that people engaged in management will find this book useful for their day-to-day activities. The Management is not a subject of experts' interest only, but also to common people, both men and women will learn much from it.

May this book inspire people to become a better person. These are my last words and I am now closing my eyes.

INTENSIVE CARE UNIT
Medical College,
Lucknow

Narayanji Misra

The author while writing this book was under continuous pain of abdomen cancer which could not be detected in spite of the best medical support available at Kanpur.
Before the author could complete the last chapter, he was admitted in Medical College Hospital, Lucknow in the third stage of cancer, of which he died after 21 days.

Contents

Prologue

The Manager

When the word 'manager' is used, the picture that emerges in our mind is that of a professional manager. But, the persons who manage the affairs, maybe of a family, a shop, an office and a variety of other such places or activities are also managers in their own right. Therefore, the qualities leading to managerial excellence assume relevance not only for the professionals but also for all those who are engaged in the task of managing any place of work or activity.

Indian Scriptures

Management has been much talked about, discussed and deliberated upon in the present century. Its wide scope has been identified, realised and recognised. There have been various thinkers and managers of repute who have made significant contributions to this discipline. Numerous thoughts and theories have been propounded, tried and practised. Nevertheless, the prudence shrouded in Indian scriptures remains par excellence. The wisdom talked about so far back in time is as relevant today as the modern thoughts. Thanks to the sagacity of some modern scholars, thinkers and practitioners as well that the age-old wisdom can now be seen, practised and experienced. They are no more hidden or considered as archaic. These thoughts are well described, explained and have been authenticated by a load of experience. Therefore, they are valuable and practical. The modern thoughts are very close to them and it appears that they draw heavily from them.

The Vedas

Vedas tell about *Dharma*, which according to Julius Jolly is, "One of the most comprehensive and important term in the whole range of Sanskrit literature". The connotation and the soul of the term '*Dharma*' is much wider than its usual rendering, the 'Religion'. *Dharma* stands for the whole range of duties of mankind, the performance of which is conducive to human welfare. *Dharma*, therefore, constitutes the duties of the people towards self and the society. They have, for that reason, been propounded through the Vedic injunctions. It has been said:

> स्वस्तिपन्था मनुचरेम सूर्याचन्द्रमसाविव।
> पुनर्ददताऽघ्नता जानता सं गमेमहि।।
>
> (Svastipanthā manucarem suryācandramasāviva
> Punardadtāghnatā jānatā saḿ gamemahi)
>
> — *Rig Veda (5-51-15)*
>
> *May we ever unswervingly follow the path of duty as do the sun and the moon! May we always serve humanity without demanding the price of our service! May we ever be benevolent, kind, self-sacrificing, detached and adjustable! May we surrender all and serve humanity like the sun and the moon!*

Following the Vedic tradition, the *Rishis* (sages), the thinkers and scholars have also laid down the duties of all classes, creeds and professions. It is from these that the people following different professions can draw their relevant prudence. That is how thc 'managerial wisdom' has been identified.

The Sages

The sages, *gurus* (teachers) and scholars like Śukra, Brihaspati, Yajňyavalkya, Nārad, Vedavyāsa, Manu, Kautilya, Bhartrihari and a host of others have elaborated the duties to be performed for the welfare of the mankind and society. These writings, inter alia contain the matters of interest to the managers (professional and otherwise), which constitute managerial skills. Proper understanding, assimilation and practice of such knowledge from the scriptures have a high potential for improving the quality of managers in general and also in particular.

General Duties

Being specific about the duties, Kautilya has prescribed six general duties for all citizens. These duties are:

सर्वेषामहिंसा सत्यं शौचमनसूया नृशंस्यं क्षमा च ।

(Sarveṣāmhiṁsā satyaṁ śaucamansūyā nṛśsya kṣmā ca)

— *Artha Śastra (1-3-3)*

Abstaining from injury to living creatures, following the path of truthfulness, uprightness, freedom from malice, compassion and forbearance are the six duties for all citizens.

Abstaining from injury to living creatures includes both physical as well as verbal injury. Use of humiliating words, abusive phrases and sarcastic remarks are some of the verbal injuries, which are equally hurting and killing as physical injuries. These are all forbidden as a part of the duties.

Truth is to be practised in a way that only the pleasant truth be spoken. The injunction does not mean that one may tell pleasant lies but refrain from speaking unpleasant truth. Wisdom suggests that one may better keep quiet rather than speak lies.

Honest dealing is always liked by everyone. An upright person always engages himself in clear and honest dealings. Thus he is bold, imposing and wields considerable influence.

One who practises freedom from malice does not bear any grudge against anyone. So, as a part of duty, one should not nurse any grudge or ill will for anyone, but should rather discuss the matter and see the end of it.

Compassion is a shade higher than kindness or mercy. The one having compassion nurses soft feelings for others. A compassionate person is necessarily kind-hearted, benevolent, merciful and loving.

Forbearance too is a fundamental duty. A person having forbearance abstains from vices. He possesses a lot of patience and command over his temper and is merciful as well.

The duties prescribed by Kautilya are the virtues. So, in a way, he prescribes that the fundamental duties of citizens are to be virtuous.

Prescribing general duties of citizens is, though a concept of the past, but is also equally modern. Part IV A (Article 51A) of the Constitution of India also lays down the 'Fundamental Duties of Citizens'.

Thought Management

The learning from the scriptures needs to be taken up with special understanding, the basic reason being that they have built-in difficulties, which cater to a well-organised thought management process. The thought process is so activated that the understanding capacity gets vitalised, which is necessary to sharpen the intellect. One of the important purposes is to develop and sharpen the thinking capacity of the reader. As the *Kath-Upanishad* rightly says:

उत्तिष्ठत जाग्रत प्राप्य वरान्निबोधत्।

(Úttiśthat jāgrat prāpya varānnibodhat)

— *Kath-Upanishad (1-3-14)*

Get up, be awake and find thy goal.

The thought gets provoked whether a person in sleep gets up first and then wakes up or vice-versa. The purpose is to make the reader think and then come to correct conclusion — the true meaning. The thought needs to be managed, as this is an effective way of learning. The thought process requires to be tuned up to understand the real intent. If the reader catches the clue, the difficulty fades out. Just a little thought is required and the meaning bccomes easy. 'Get up' (उत्तिष्ठत) in this context means, get involved in work and 'be awake' (जाग्रत) means, be attentive towards the goal. So the meaning is, start the work, get involved, be attentive towards the goal and attain success.

Symbolic Presentation

The other aspect that ought to be kept in view while studying the scriptures is that the reader may attune himself with the symbolic presentation. Very important matters have been symbolically explained, for example in the last *śloka* (couplet) of *Srimad Bhagvat Gita*, wherein Krishna signifies the *atman* (soul) and Partha (Arjuna) stands for the 'physical body'. In another interpretation, Krishna may represent the mental power and Arjuna the muscle power.

Correct Meaning of Words

The words used in the various Indian scriptures are often multifaceted and have more than one meaning. Thus, it becomes all the more important to interpret them as per the context. If that is not done, the conclusion may be faulty. For example, the Sanskrit word *danda* (दण्ड) may mean punishment, the laws, the administration, and so on according to the context. Therefore, the scripture texts need a special approach for their proper understanding.

Attaining Objectives

Every manager has a goal to achieve and has resources at his disposal. He has to plan, coordinate, motivate and control the available resources and attain the goal despite all constraints. In the process, he has to win over all the difficulties, manage crises and keep persevering. If, despite all efforts, the success eludes, he has to look for the shortcomings that might have remained. The Sanskrit saying goes:

> यत्ने कृते यदि न सिध्यति कोऽत्र दोषः ।
> (Yatne kṛte yadi na siddhyati koatra dòshaḥ)
>
> *If, in spite of all efforts, success is not achieved, some fault has remained somewhere.*

The Vedic Views

In the matter of attaining the objectives, the physical resources alone do not assume prime importance. The real important factors are firm resolve, consistent efforts and adhering fairly and firmly to the set policies. In this context, the *Rig Veda* says:

> पादृश्मिन्घायि तमपस्यया विवद ।
> (Pàdṛśminghàyi tampasyayá vivad)
>
> — *Rig Veda (5-44-8)*
>
> *Verily you win the blessings of the Lord if your heart is set on a definite objective. If there is firm resolve then with efforts, the success is a must. Sincerity of purpose helps attainment of goal.*

For sincere efforts, the same 'ṛca' (ऋचा) says:

य उ स्वयं वहते सो अरे करत्।

(Ya u svayaṁ vahate so are karat)

— *Rig Veda (5-44-8)*

One attains the goal through one's own efforts.

Sukra's Views — Firm Policies

Adhering fairly and firmly to the set policies is the third component of success achievement; Śukra says:

अनीतिरेव साच्छिद्रं राज्ञो नित्यं भयावहम।
शत्रुसंवर्धनं प्रोक्तं बलह्रासकरं महत।।

(Anītirev sācchidram rājño nityam bhayāvaham
śatrusaṁvardhanaṁ proktam balhrāskram mahat)

— *Śukra Nitih (1-15)*

Being without a policy is the greatest deficiency of an administrator, as it is fearsome, increases enemies and diminishes his own force (powers).

So, the administrator ought to have set policies and should act *according to them fairly and firmly.*

Mental and Physical Health

According to the *Rig Veda*, there is one more pre-requisite besides the physical resources. It has been said:

अव स्थिरा तनुहि भूरि शर्धतां।

(Ava sthirā tanuhi bhuri śardhtāṁ)

— *Rig Veda (8-19-20)*

A healthy mind and a strong body are the first requisites to achieve the desired goal.

It must be kept into consideration that a healthy body has a healthy mind. When we talk about maintaining the health, it not only means bodily health but includes mental health as well.

Stage for Study is Set

Such inputs bring us to a stage from where we can proceed for the study of Indian scriptures, understand and appreciate and then assimilate them for practice. The scriptures are affluent so far the theories and practice of art and science of management are concerned. It will further be visible that the principles and thoughts enunciated so far back in the past appear to be fresh and are relevant, even in the modern times. That justifies the study.

OO

1

The Basic Managerial Functions

Managerial Functions

Management is a multifunctional affair, involving various skills and niceties. However, there are four basic functions involved, namely planning, coordinating, motivating and controlling the resources for attainment of goal. These functions represent the modern thought currently in-vogue. Though, these functions are modern, they have their roots deep into the past.

Planning

Ancient Indian thinkers, scholars and sages deliberated upon the said four functions, the testimony of which is borne by the Indian scriptures.

Planning, the first amongst the managerial activities had drawn the attention of the composer of the epic *Mahabharata* in these words:

> कृत्यानि पूर्वं परिसंख्याय सर्वाण्यायव्यये चानुरूपां च वृत्तिम् ।
> संगृहीण्यादनुरूपान सहायान सहायसाध्यानि हि दुष्कराणि ।।
> (Kṛityāni pūrvam parisankhyāy sarvā nyāyavyaye cānurūpāṁ ca vrittim
> Sangṛhinyādanurūpāṁ sahāyān sahāyasadhyāni hi duşkrāni)
> — *Mahabharata Udyog Parva (37-24)*

In the beginning, the exact dimensions of the work, the budget, the reasonable wages etc should be looked into, decided and settled. Thereafter, able and qualified helpers should be recruited for the reason that even the toughest work can be accomplished with the assistance of competent helpers.

In the above *śloka*, though the human resource has been considered the last priority, has still been given the top preference for the reasons that all can be done with the help of suitable helpers. Of course, the order in which the feasibility of work has to be examined, the higher priority goes to the work dimensions. All the factors vary to a large extent according to the dimensions of the assignment. The assignment decides the budget and the type of workforce needed, their wage rates and procurement. Howsoever lavish the budget may be, but the goal can be attained only with the help of suitable personnel.

There are four steps in between the goal and its realisation, namely, the budget, decision about reasonable wages, the quality, qualifications and procurement of competent workforce. All these steps depend upon planning, the foremost among all managerial functions.

Planned Use of Resources

The resources can be made available adequately or in abundance but most important is the manager, with suited acumen. This is a rare talent. Śukra, in this context, has said:

अमंत्रमक्षरं नास्ति नास्ति मूलम नौषधं।
अयोज्ञः पुरूषो नास्ति योजकस्तत्र दुर्लभः ।।
(Amantram akṣram nāsti nāsti mūlam naushdham
Ayojnaḥ puruṣo nāsti yogakastatra durlabhaḥ)

— *Śukra Nitih (2-127)*

There is no alphabet that cannot be used as a 'mantra', no root or herb that cannot be used as a medicine, no man is useless or good for nothing, but rare is the planner and user of these resources — the manager.

The letters (in the alphabet), by themselves have no value. Yet, their hidden strength is so great that purposefully combined together, they can constitute powerful 'mantras'. The roots and shrubs are not of much value till their potential is identified. After identification of their potential, they can be used as medicines and wonder drugs many a times. In the same way, men and women after being properly trained can be transformed into a resource. Thus, there is no man or woman who is not capable of being used as a resource provided he is placed with a manager who knows how to use the human resource.

Manager who is the planner for the use of the resources is a rare gem. It depends upon the ingenuity of the manager how he can use the resources in the most suitable and optimum manner. He is the one who ought to possess the knowledge and the knack for correct and optimum use of the resources.

Planning and Time Management

The scope of the planning activity is wide enough. Time, the most precious resource needs a planned use. Indian thinkers and sages were conscious of this important factor. *Mahabharata* says:

> निश्चित्य यः प्रक्रमते नान्तर्वसति कर्मणः ।
> अवन्ध्यकालो वश्यात्मा सवै पण्डित उच्यते । ।
> (Niścitya yaḥ prakramate nāntrvasti karmanaḥ
> Avandhykālo vaśyātmā sa vai pandit ucayate)
>
> — *Mahabharata Udyog Parva (3-24)*
>
> *One, who first decides and plans the work and then starts it, does not stop in between, does not waste time and remains fully attentive, has self-control is called a learned person.*

Ability of a manager lies first in planning how the work is to be done and how best the resources can be utilised. It is after such planning that he starts the work and then keeps going, without wasting or misusing time, attains the goal and operates with full control over his senses. He never gets distracted or discouraged.

This observation shows a perfect example of planning and optimum use of the resources, especially the time. This also deals with the coordination activity of management.

Modern thinkers on management have evolved many theories on planning in general and time management in particular. Peter F. Drucker has made substantial contribution to the theory of time management. In spite of such theories and wisdom being available, a number of projects do not get completed within the specified time frame. This leads to loss of budgetary control and competitors taking advantage.

Work when started needs complete attention of not only the manager but also his team. If there is no coordination, complete attention, and appropriate motivation, it may not be possible to attain objectives within the fixed time frame. It is only a wise manager, who knows the tricks of the trade and succeeds.

Time Budgeting

The aforesaid thought about planning and its execution in a time bound manner is further reinforced by Śukra, who in the context of time budgeting, has said:

> कालं नियम्य कार्याणि ह्याचरेन्नान्यथा क्वचित।
> (Kālaṁ niyamya kāryāni hyācrennanyathā kvacit)
>
> — *Śukra Nitih (3-296)*

> *Work should be done in a time bound manner. One should not act contrary to this.*

In this statement, the injunctive approach is such that command and prohibition are welded together. The command being that target must be achieved within a time schedule, the prohibition is that no work should exceed the time limit planned.

This concept of time budgeting and audit conceived by Śukra, though age-old wisdom is modern as well. Exceeding the time budget may at times be suicidal for the reasons that:

- The monetary budget may get escalated as the price rise calls for more money,
- Time schedule for other products may get disturbed,
- Competitors may come in the market with improved product,
- Loss of revenue that would have been earned if the product had been in the market in time,
- Complicated labour and industrial problems may crop-up, and
- Market trend may change and may give rise to many other problems.

Periodical time audit is for control over the time budget for which review of the progress becomes essential. Wise managers do the time planning before initiating a project. The purpose of the aforesaid injunctions is that the managers may take up a strict time planning and stick to that.

Coordination

Since management is multifunctional, the managers are called upon to establish suitable coordination between different disciplines. If a person is the manager of a particular department, he, in his functioning ought to coordinate with other departments.

Deliberating upon coordination, Nārad has said:

कच्चिन्मन्त्रयसे नैकः कच्चिन्न बहुभिः सह।
कच्चित्ते मन्त्रितो मन्त्रो न राष्ट्रं परिधावति।।

(Kaccinmntrayse naikaḥ kaccinna bahubhih sah,
kaccitte mantrito mantro narāṣtraṁ paridhāvati)

Do you take decisions on your own (alone)? Do you consult more than one person on secret matters? Do your secret matters (issues) get known to one and all?

Nārad has often adopted a questioning style for propounding a thought. In the above couplet, he has advised that decisions should not be taken by an administrator on his own. He ought to take the decision with the advice of able persons. The decisions on important secret matters should not be divulged to many persons. The administrator ought to seek advice from a cross-section of the people in such a way that the decision so taken may not become public.

The four managerial functions, namely planning, coordinating, motivating and controlling are so closely knit that they tend to overlap one another. What was true in the ancient period equally holds good even today. The managerial functions are such that they have to be followed religiously for accomplishing any task. It can hardly be claimed by anyone that he/she could do something solely on his own. Help and coordination must be sought from someone, somewhere. Moreover, coordination alone is not of much help, unless there is some motivation. Motivation does not come so late. In fact, it acts at different stages.

Motivation

One important managerial obligation is to motivate the people constituting the workforce. How can it be done, has been deliberated upon thus:

यथा गुणान्स्व भृत्यांश्च प्रजा संरंजयन्नृपः ।
शाखा पदानतः कांश्चिद परम् फलदानतः ।।
अन्यान् सुचक्षुषा हास्यैस्तथा कोमलया गिरा ।।
(Yathā gunānsva bhṛtyārśca prajā sanranjayayennṛpaḥ
śākhā padāntah kānścid parān phaldānataḥ
Anyān sacaujnuṣā hāsyaistathā komalyā girā)

— *Śukra Nitih (2-421)*

The King (substitute it by 'employer' or 'manager') should preserve the virtues of the employees, make appropriate, ordinary or higher rewards and keep them encouraged with sweet looks and soft words, and thus serve the people.

Motivate Performers

This high virtue in the area of human relations and motivation is attained when the manager has keen and watchful sight to evaluate the worth of the employees. He ought to be able to identify the star performers and reward their performance, so that the employees get encouraged and motivated. But the question remains as to what the rewards can be. Again rewards cannot be given every day, so what remains the motivator on such days. This gap can be filled by the sweet looks and soft words of the manager. It is by this means that the employees can be won over. Such manager is respected and possesses high personal power.

High and sincere performance needs to be rewarded, if not otherwise then with appreciation. The thought relevant is:

कच्चित्पुरुषकारेण पुरुषः कर्म शोभयन् ।
लभते मानमधिकं भूयो वा भक्त वेतनम् ।।
(Kaccitpuruṣkāren puruṣaḥ karma śobhayan
Labhate mānmadhikam bhuyo vābhaktavetanam)

— *Nārad Nitih (53)*

Do the people doing better and sincere work get higher respect, recognition and wages?

Nārad in his own style issues injunction and advice. He asks a question, the reply of which is to be sought. The prudence suggested is practical. The employers must perceive that providing high rewards for high performance acts as an ace motivator in many ways.

Motivation to Intellectuals

The next question talks further about motivation, thus:

> कच्चिद्विद्याविनीतांश्च नरांज्ञानविशारदान् ।
> यर्थाहं गुणतश्चैव दानेनाऽभ्युपपद्यसे । ।
> (Kaccidvidyāvinitānśca narānjňāna viśārdān
> Yāthārhaṁ guntaścaiva dānenābhupapadyaśe)
>
> — *Nārad Nitih (54)*

Do the literary persons and intellectuals get rewarded according to their merits?

This question suggests that the persons doing the work of a higher order ought to be suitably rewarded. The literary persons and the intellectuals do the work of a fairly high order as compared to those who work with physical labour. Therefore, Nārad opines that their performance must be rewarded. Thus, he suggests incentive and motivation for performing the work of higher skill. This may be in the shape of higher wages, more benefits, greater respect or recognition commensurate with their nature and performance.

Motivation for Heroic Deeds

Then again a question connected with motivation comes up is:

> काच्चिदारान्मनुष्याणां तवाऽर्थे मृत्युमीयुषाम ।
> व्यसनं चाऽभ्युपेतानां विभर्षि भरतर्षभ । ।
> (Kaccidārānmanuşyānāṁ tavārthe mrityumīyuşām
> vyasanam caābhupetānām vibharşi bhrataşbha)
>
> — *Nārad Nitih (55)*

Do you take care of those who lay their lives for your cause or get into danger?

Here, Nārad pleads that the workers who are sincere and totally devoted to the organisation should be treated with utmost care and indulgence. When the worker perceives such attitude of the employer, he is immensely motivated to put his life and soul for the organisation. In a way, this is a social security measure but also works as a motivator.

Conclusion

The four basic managerial functions are such that the thinkers and practitioners of all times must contribute their thoughts and theories to these functions. The ancient thinkers, as we know, have made rich contributions. Kautilya has also suggested incentive bonus for those workers who produce more than the targets fixed for them.

The contribution of ancient Indian thinkers suggests that they had a clear vision of such functions and their respective importance. Here again they may be taken as forerunners of the modern thought.

OO

2

Self Development

Essential Qualities of Manager

A manager ought to know the workers who constitute his workforce. Nonetheless, his higher responsibility is to know his own self and so also the challenges that he has to face. The qualities that any person ought to possess in order to be a successful and effective manager have been enumerated in *Mahabharata* as:

आत्मज्ञानं समारम्भस्तितीक्षा धर्मनित्यता ।
यमर्थान्नापकर्षन्ति स वै पण्डित उच्यते । ।

(Ātmajnānam samārambhastitīkṣā dharmanityatā
yamrthānnapakṣranti sa vai pandit ucayate)

— *Mahabharata Udyog Parva (33-16)*

The person who possesses the knowledge of his real self, has capacity to bear the agony, remain engaged in performance of duty and is never distracted is called a 'pandit', a learned one.

The couplet above makes a direct mention of four qualities and two can be read in between the lines. These are:

- Knowledge about self, which results into self-development,
- Knowledge about the people in his team,
- Acting as a model for his workforce,
- Engaging his own self and his team in assignments and keep making constant efforts,
- Possessing capacity to bear pain of failures and criticism, and

- Remaining whole-heartedly engaged in performance of his duties (*Dharma*).

Thus, a manager ought to be blended with many qualities. The one possessing the aforesaid qualities increases his personal power. Nevertheless, there are many other qualities that a manager needs to possess. One of them is 'listening habits'.

Manager's Listening Habits

Besides being a good talker, a successful manager must be a good listener as well. The more a manager listens, the better informed he becomes. He gets more time to think and resolve the problems. In the matter of listening habits, it has been said:

क्षिप्रं विजानाति चिरं श्रृणोति विज्ञाय चार्थं भजते न कामात।
नासम्पृष्टो व्युपयुक्तें पदार्थे तत प्रज्ञानं प्रथमं पण्डितस्य।।

(Kṣiprám vijānāti ciram śrinoti
vijñaya cartham bhajate na kāmāt
Nāsampristo vyupyumkte padārthe
tata prajñānaṁ prathaṁ panditasya)

— *Mahabharata Udyog Parva (33-22)*

A learned and wise person listens for long and completely, understands quickly, indulges in action and does not express views about anyone without listening to a person.

Patience in listening, works wonders many a times. It wears out an angry person of his anger. Explaining by an example, a man who had grievances pending since long, got fed up and ultimately decided to call on the Chief Minister and abuse him so that he may be sent to the jail where he would get at least two meals a day. Somehow he managed to appear before the Chief Minister. He started using harsh and abusive language. The security men wanted to whisk away the man, but the Chief Minister asked them not to do so and let the man speak to his full. The man again, narrating his grievances, abused the Chief Minister. He continued and was not checked till he got tired, slowed down and finally was quiet, waiting for his arrest order. At this juncture, the Chief Minister called his Private Secretary. In soft and sympathetic words, he directed him to personally look into the case of that man to get the grievances redressed within a week and let him (the Chief Minister) know about that. With such humane behaviour, the angry man, broke down completely and started weeping and repenting for his behaviour.

The story was soon widely known and the public servants became alert. Such is the magic of patient listening.

However, listening alone is not enough. Listening and understanding should go together. Manager should be quick at understanding the issue correctly. Then, he should act fast to resolve the issue and get the desired result.

The *śloka* also deals with the issue of forming opinions. At times, the manager forms an opinion about a subordinate on the basis of hearsay alone. This is not a fair deal. The rule is that none should be condemned unheard. Therefore, forming an opinion about anyone, without hearing him on that matter may not be fair. Any opinion must be based on authenticity, reasonably and not in an arbitrary manner. One of the most important qualities of a good manager is that he must act in a judicious and unbiased manner. One must appreciate that the authority needs to be used carefully.

Power Corrupts

Authority is a very attractive weapon; but if it is not used fairly, it may lead the person to disrepute for the reason that authority often tends to corrupt. In this context, Śukra has said:

अधिकार मदं पीत्वा को न मुह्येत्पुनश्चिरम् ।
अतः कार्यश्रमं दृष्ट्वा कार्येऽन्ये तं नियोजयेत ।।

(Adhikar madaḿ pītva ko na muhyetpumaściram
Ataḥ karya kşmaḿ dŗştva karyeanyetam niyojyet)

— *Śukra Nitih (2-114)*

Whom does the authority not intoxicate? Therefore, one should not be allowed to wield authority for very long. In consideration of the ability, a person should be shifted to another job.

A saying goes, "Power corrupts absolute power absolutely." Śukra gave a similar idea centuries back and in a more practical manner, he provided a workable solution as well. The solution is that no one should be allowed to remain in authority for a long period. The persons in authority should be transferred to other positions on the basis of their abilities. Yet this may not be called an absolute view. If a person in authority does not show any signs of corruption, he may continue in that position for long.

In this situation, monetary misdealing should not be the only factor to be considered. It also needs to be seen if the person in authority acts judiciously.

Inaction and Over Action

If the person in authority gets swollen headed and starts acting arbitrarily on his whims and caprices, this may go on for some time but not always, for the basic reason that such conduct is perceived as foolish acts. Deliberating in this context, an old Sanskrit saying is:

अनाचारस्तु मालिन्यम्, अत्याचारस्तु मूर्खता: ।

(Anācārasytu mālinyam, atyācārastu mūrkhtāḥ)

While inaction is sterile, over action and arbitrary action are irrational and foolish.

This message is of utmost importance for the administrators including managers. For example, not taking any action when misconduct comes to notice is inaction. On the other hand, dealing with even minor misconducts with a very heavy hand or awarding excessive punishments tends to be over action. The relevant saying is:

अति सर्वत्र वर्जयेत् ।

(Ati sarvatra varjayet)

Excess of everything is bad.

Therefore, if any corrective action is needed, that will be to adopt a balanced approach. An administrator indulging in inaction or over action tends to cause serious annoyance to the affected people. Creating an army of unsatisfied people may not surface the harm in a short period. Nevertheless that annoyance remains like a sparkle of fire for some time and may assume serious proportions in the long run. Cautioning on this point, Kautilya has given a formula:

नास्त्यग्ने दौर्बल्यम् ।

(Nastyagne daurblyam)

— *Chanakya Sūtram (88)*

Who can call the fire weak?

This formula gives the message through a question.

Think of the answer and the smoke clears up.

Fire is a powerful element of the nature. It is a great friend of the mankind. At the same time, it can cause serious devastations too. In no way, fire can be said to be weak. And what is true of fire is equally true of enemy — the opponent. A minute particle of fire can assume serious proportions; similarly even a single enemy can cause serious damages. This hard fact must be understood fully well by the managers. They ought to have a clear understanding that if, by their arbitrary action, they create a large number of discontented subordinates, at one time or the other, they can land into difficult situations. Therefore, the message and advice from the formula is that an administrator or a manager, by his thoughtless action, should not create a number of unsatisfied people, as much depends on the numbers.

Majority the Most Strong

A large number of people create and change the public opinion. It must be appreciated by the managers that public opinion is very powerful. Śukra, in this context, has said:

बहुनामैकमत्यं हि नृपतेर्बलवत्तरम् ।
बहुसूचकृतो रज्जुः सिंहाद्याकर्षण क्षमः ।

(Bahunamaikamatyaṁ hi nṛpaterbalavattaram
Bahusutrakrito rajjuḥ sinhadyakarşana kşamaḥ)

— *Śukra Nitih (4-7-419)*

The majority opinion is stronger than the King. The King too has to bow down before it. It is like a rope made of numerous threads that develop the capacity to pull a lion as well.

The idea underlying the couplet is much significant. People like Jawaharlal Nehru have very much appreciated Śukra for the thought. The message that the thought gives is that no such policy may be pursued or action taken which may not be liked by the majority of people. Such policy or action cannot last long; on the contrary, it may create various problems. Therefore, it is wise to assess the situation before launching any important policy or action.

Announce Only When Work is Complete

Chanakya, the great administrator of foresight, has given a crisp formula in this context:

सिद्धस्यैव कार्यस्य प्रकाशनं कर्तव्यं ।

(Siddhasyaiva kāryasya prakāśnaṁ kartavyaṁ)

— *Chanakya Sūtram (121)*

Only that work should be made known, which has been accomplished.

For successful timing and managing well, the thought propounded in the above *sūtram* is very useful and practical too. Some relevant points are:

- If a product is in the manufacturing stage and its knowledge goes out, the competitors may plan a better quality product and capture the market with something much ahead of the product of the original manufacturer,
- In case of any failures, the person or team making it may tend to face demoralisation,
- Some industrial problem may creep in,
- Spiritually, it is believed that evil forces attack and create hindrances, and
- People engaged in manufacture are likely to get inert due to the feeling that the item would come out as planned in any case.

The wisdom contained in the above said formula has been reinforced by Nārad as well, who has said:

काच्चिद्राजन्कृतान्येव कृतप्रायाणि वा पुनः ।
विदुस्ते वीर कर्माणि ननिवाप्नानि कानिचित् ।।

(Kaccidrājnkṛtānyeva kṛtprāyāni vā punaḥ
viduste vīr karmāni nānvāpnāni kānicit)

— *Nārad Nitih (33)*

Do the unfinished acts of yours get known? Do your unfinished assignments get known to one and all? Do the people know only your unaccomplished assignments?

The above couplet completely confirms that any work should be made public only when that is done. Thus wisdom is very relevant in industry and politics.

Avail Opportunity Promptly

However it also needs to be kept in view that a person must keep alert all along and be prepared to encash the opportunity as soon as it comes, because opportunities do not come frequently. Kautilyan view in this behalf is:

कालश्च सकृदभ्येति य नरं कालकांक्षिणम ।
दुर्लभः स पुनस्तस्य कालं कर्म चिकीर्षतः । ।
(Kālaśca sakṛdbhyeti ya naram kālkānkṣinam
durlabhaḥ sa punastasya kalam karm cikirṣatah)

— *Artha Śastra (2-6-31)*

Time comes but once to a man waiting for an opportunity. Such time is difficult for that man to get again when he wants to do the work.

No Dependence on Fate

Any opportunity coming the way should be encashed without any dependence on fate. The reason being that it was the fate that brought that chance, and making proper use of that depends upon the man alone. There is no scope for moods as moods too are man's own creation. Thus, wisdom demands that opportunities should be promptly utilised. Yet, there are persons who trust in stars and fate alone, about whom, Kautilya has said:

दैव प्रमाणो मानुषहीनो निरारम्भो ।
विपन्नकर्मारम्भो वाऽवसीदति । ।
(Daiva pramāno mānuṣhino nirārambho
Vipannakarmārambho vāvasīdati)

— *Artha Śastra (7-11-34)*

One trusting only in fate, being devoid of human endeavour, perishes, because either he does not start his undertakings or assignments, or miscarries them.

Kautilya, being an action-oriented thinker, believed in human endeavour. He himself struggled throughout his life. Therefore, it was befitting for him to think that a person believing in fate alone, perishes. The one depending on fate tends to suffer from inertia, which checks his activities. In the process, he becomes completely broken and decays in due course.

A wise person is the one who knows that if even the stars have to act, they will need a functionary. So the prudent one will have to be alert to become an instrument of the stars and encash each opportunity that comes by. It is necessary to clearly understand that despite failures, one must always continue to strive for the obvious reason that a failure today may lead to success tomorrow.

Sadhana

Besides the stars, a section of people believe in *prārabdha* (प्रारब्ध) (the inherited situation, condition or tendency). Nevertheless, they ought to understand that *puruśārtha* (पुरुषार्थ) or efforts can change the *prārabdha*. Remaining active in the midst of the play between *prārabdha* and *puruśārtha* is *sadhana* (साधना) or the endeavour to get a particular result. For example, a person is a left-hander by birth, which may be said to be his *prārabdha*. If he is determined to be right-handed and makes all the efforts, he might become a right-hander one day. So by *puruśārtha*, anyone can attain his goals. This process of changing the *prārabdha* by *puruśārtha* is the *sadhana*. It needs to be clearly understood that the *sadhana* with full faith in *puruśārtha* assumes great importance in the lives of those who strive for attaining objectives.

Virtues to be used as per Principles

Puruśārtha carries the greatest potential for attaining even the most difficult objectives. This is the process by which, some have changed or amended their behaviour. High virtues, like peace, goodwill and welfare etc, can be gained by *puruśārtha* or continuous endeavour.

Attaining such virtues is possible but their use requires a specialised wisdom. If not used properly, they are likely to portray a different picture of the person using them. For example, display of humility before an evil person may be perceived as weakness. A weak person talking in a peaceful manner is taken to be an act of cowardice and so on. Cautioning in this behalf, Kautilya has said:

> *संध्यादीनाम यथोद्देशः वस्थापनमपनयः तस्मादपदः संम्भवन्ति ।*
> (Sandhyādinām yathoddeśah vasthāpana mapanyaḥ.
> tasmāpadadah sambhavanti)
>
> — *Artha Śastra (9-50)*

Use of peaceful and humble behaviour not in a prescribed manner is a wrong policy. From that springs the dangers of conspiracy and revolt.

'Prescribed' here does not mean that Kautilya has prescribed some method. It means a recognised manner. For example, Sukra has deliberated upon the four strategies of winning over people. No doubt, the virtues are of high value but if they are inappropriately used, difficulties may come up.

Adopting the virtues by *puruśārtha* is good, but their darker side can also not be ignored. *Mahabharata* also cautions on this issue:

एक एव दमे दोषो द्वितीयो नापपद्यते।
यदेन क्षमया युक्तमशक्तं मन्यते जनः ।।

(Eak eva dame doşo dvitiyo nappadyate
ydena kşamaya yuktamaśaktaṁ manyate janaḥ)

— *Mahabharata Shanti Parva (160-34)*

Self-restraint has only one defect not a second one that because of the forgiveness people consider it a weakness.

Self-restraint also needs that the person practising it must be strong. It is a virtue that ought to be used for the self development and spreading goodwill.

A person practising self-restraint without adopting necessary precautions and proper understanding may create complications for his own self and for others as well.

A manager practising self-restraint will be a noble person. Yet, if he gives that soft impression to one and all, some of his subordinates may start taking liberties. Therefore, the better course of action for him may be to mould his personality in a manner that he may be full of compassion and kindness from within but outwardly he must give a look of strict and strong person and that calls for the theory of distance.

Theory of Distances

A manager ought to be conversant with the 'theory of distances'. A mother has love and compassion for her children, but she must also give the looks of strictness. A mother ought to possess the heart of a cow, but her looks must be that of a lion. She has love for the children, yet maintains a respectable distance from them. An effective manager must maintain such distance from the subordinates. He should be the champion of welfare of the subordinates, yet need not be chummy with them. A respectable distance must always be maintained, so that they may not dare to take undue liberties with him.

Closing Remarks

Before closing this chapter, it may be useful to consider a piece of advice from *Mahabharata*:

> सर्पान् कुशाग्राणि तथोपदानं ज्ञाता मनुष्याः परिवर्जयन्ति।
> अज्ञानतस्तत्र पतन्ति केचिज्ज्ञाने फलं पश्यं यथा विशिष्टम।।
>
> (Sarpān kuśāgrāni tathopadānaṁ
> Jňāta manuşyāḥ parivarjayanti
> Ajnānatastatra patanti keci jiňāne
> phalam paśya yatha viśiştam)
>
> — *Mahabharata – Shanti Parva*
> – *Mokshadharma Parva (201-22)*

When one knows that there are snakes, thorns and wells in the way then he should go that way avoiding those obstacles. Yet there are many who do not know and fall on them. Therefore have a look at the importance of knowledge.

The message hidden in this *śloka* of *Mahabharata* is that one must possess fair knowledge of the way he has to tread, so as to have the knowledge about all the dangers and the obstacles.

The one who takes up managerial position must be fully acquainted with the challenges and the prudence required for the profession. One who takes care of this aspect emerges out as a successful and efficient manager.

OO

3

Cultivate Your Workforce

Worker the Most Important Resource

Mahabharata pronounces a great wisdom by saying:

> सहाय साध्यानि हि दुष्कराणि ।
> (Sahāya sādhyāni hi duśkrāni)
>
> — *Mahabharata Udyog Parva (37-24)*
>
> *Difficult works can all be accomplished with the assistance of competent helpers.*

So, a prudent manager takes great care of his subordinates. Their dignity, morale, grievances and problems assume high priority in his agenda.

Human Dignity

The preamble of the Constitution of India promises to secure to all the citizens, 'Fraternity, assuming the dignity of individual and the unity and integrity of the Nation'.

The Article 21 of the Constitution provides further protection of life and personal liberty. This protection of the life has been interpreted as 'life with human dignity' by the Supreme Court of India in many cases.

— *Bandhua Mukti Morcha versus Union of India 1984(3) section 161 and many other cases*

Thus human dignity assumes the highest place amongst all human values. After retirement from active service, Field Marshal Maneckshaw was questioned by a correspondent as to what was his highest achievement of his long service career. The Field Marshal replied that his highest achievement was that his officers and men served under him with dignity. The highest reward for any person is that his/her dignity is maintained.

Indian thinkers and scholars were also very much aware of the importance of human dignity. In their opinion, the employees whose dignity has been properly upheld are more loyal and committed to the organisation. Śukra in this context has said:

भृति दानेन संतुष्टा मानेन परिवर्धिताः ।
संत्विता मृदुवाचा या न त्यजंत्यधिपं हि ते ।।

(Bhriti dānena santuṣṭā mānen parivardhitāḥ
santvitā mriduvacā ya na tyantydhipam hi te)

— *Śukra Nitih (2-419)*

Workers satisfied by the payment of wages, whose self-respect has been elevated, who have been pacified by soft words, never desert the King (employer).

People primarily work for monetary benefits. Therefore, it is necessary that they should be satisfied by the payment of wages. After the basic needs get fulfilled they crave for their self-respect, morale and dignity. They do not want to be subjected to humiliation; they need to be pacified by soft and loving words.

The Gita Views

Causing humiliation has a great negative value. In this context, *Srimad Bhagvat Gita* says:

सम्भावितस्य चाकीर्तिर्मरणादतिरिच्यते ।

(Sambhāvitasa cākirtir marānadātirecayte)

— *Srimad Bhagvat Gita (2-34)*

For a self-esteemed person, humiliation is worse than death.

These are the words of Lord Krishna himself. In *Srimad Bhagvat Gita*, he explains to Arjuna that if he desists from *Karma*, he will face humiliation, which will be worse than death. The ideas hidden in this *śloka* are so important that even the Supreme Court of India has quoted it in one of the decisions in the context of Article 21 of the Constitution.

Resolving Grievances

Dignity of subordinates can be maintained in various ways. One of them is that the grievances must be listed and timely resolved. An aggrieved employee does not remain 'a whole man'. Physically at work, mentally he is involved in his problems. It has, therefore, become a major managerial obligation to set up an effective procedure for resolving employees' grievances. In this context, the basic formula is:

सुदर्शना हि राजन् प्रजा रंजयन्ति ।
(Sudarśanā hi rājan prajā ranjayanti)

— *Chanakya Sūtram (559)*

The King, employer or manager who listens to the difficulties and problems of his people or employees keeps them satisfied.

Resolving the employees' problems is not limited only to their welfare. A contented workforce is more productive and thus beneficial to the employer as well. It matters much as to who has been instrumental in resolving employees' grievances. When the trade union takes a lead on this front, they become more powerful.

However, if the manager gives due care to the employees' grievances and gets them redressed, he assumes the role of a true leader and adds to his effectiveness. His personal power increases considerably. The subordinates respect him and are always ready to work on his dictates. On the whole, the workers are a satisfied lot. Thus, a wise manager champions the legitimate grievances of his subordinates and becomes useful to the organisation.

Keeping Promises

Together with the prompt handling of grievances, keeping the promises is also very essential. A famous saying goes, "Promises easily made are difficult to keep". Śukra, in this connection, has opined:

करिष्यामिति ते कार्यं न कुर्यात्कार्यलम्बनम् ।
द्राक्कुर्यात समर्थश्चेत्साशां दीर्घं न रक्षयेत ।।
(Karişyāmiti te kāryam na kurỳatkāryalambnam
Drākkuryāt samrthścetsānś dirgham na rakşyet)

— *Śukra Nitih (2-232)*

If one promises someone, "I will do your work", he should not delay in doing it. If one is competent, he must at once do it. Pending it for long and keep someone waiting for it is not proper.

Keeping one's promises is a virtue which one can develop himself. If a person only makes promises and does not care to fulfil them, he loses his credibility. The subordinates, peers and at times, the superiors lose respect and regard for such person. The practice of keeping the promise is wisdom in the sense that the subordinates tend to be more productive and the manager more effective.

Fit Persons for the Job — Morale Booster

Another aspect that takes care of the morale and also acts as a motivator is when a person is recruited in the area of his specialisation. The formula is:

यो यस्मिन कर्मणि कुशलस्तं तस्मिन्नेव योजयेत।

(Yo yasmin karmani kślastain tasminneva yojyet)

— *Chanakya Sūtram (117)*

A person who is specialist in some sphere should be assigned the same work.

The above principle may be accepted as a basic guide for recruitment and placement of the personnel. However, it also acts as a morale booster. Qualifications of a person may not be the guiding factor for assignment of jobs. His aptitude should be the guide for his placement. For example, one should not be assigned the teaching job unless he has an aptitude for teaching. In an interview for the post of a teacher, the applicants were asked as to how they would teach their subject in the classroom. While others explained the method, one of them, humbly got up and said, "Suppose sir, this is a classroom considering you the honourable members as pupils; I would proceed as, my dear boys, today I would teach you how to write accounts. You have so and so columns in the account book...." He had hardly talked for half a minute and the members exclaimed, "Very good. Now please sit down!" This candidate was selected for appointment to the post. This example shows how a fit person for a job gets easily identified. If such may be the mode of selection and placement, the round pegs will not find a place in the square holes. The morale of the employees goes fairly high. This kind of managerial sagacity develops star performers.

Welcome the Suggestions

Indian thinkers have always given due importance to the useful suggestions and ideas that may come from anyone. The Vedic philosophy has been:

आ नो भद्राः ऋतवे यन्तु विश्वतः ।

(Ā no bhardrāh ṛtavo yantu viśvataḥ)

— *Rig Veda (1-89-1)*

Let noble thoughts come to us from every side.

One ought not to shut oneself in his own shell. One must know that what one thinks is not always correct. It is, therefore, wise to be open-minded, and accept all that is beneficial, irrespective of the source it comes from. It is necessary that suggestion must at least be heard. Such listening in itself is a motivator.

This reminds of an anecdote related to F. W. Taylor, who has been called the 'Father of Scientific Management'. One of his subordinate worker in the brick field sometimes suggested changes in the method of work. Taylor replied bluntly, "You are not asked to think; there are other people here who are paid to do that work." Such approach is degrading and discouraging. In contrast to the Taylorian approach, Kautilya has said:

न कंचिदवमन्येत सर्वस्य श्रृणुयान्मतम् ।
बालस्याप्यर्थ तद्वाक्यमुपयुंजीत पण्डितः ।।

(Na kancidvamanyet sarvasya śrinuyantma
balasyapyarth tadvakyampyunjit panditaḥ)

— *Artha Śastra (1-15-22)*

Wise people should despise none. One should listen to the opinion of everybody and make use of the sensible words of even a child.

This openness of accepting good advice (suggestions) from everyone is an age-old speciality of Indians. Later, some of the western thinkers and practitioners, like Robert Owen (1771-1858), Mary Follett (1868-1933) and some others, practised the same policy with success. This thought is quite practical as 'the wearer of the shoe alone knows where it pinches'. Workers are in a better position to make suggestions for work improvement. It forms the basis for the success of Quality Circles Movement. The thought about considering suggestions goes to the extent that:

बालार्दप्यर्थजातं श्रृणुयात।

(Bālārdpyarthjātam śṛnuyāt)

— *Chanakya Sūtram (167)*

Reasonable suggestions even of children should be accepted.

Suggestions from a young one are not liable to be ignored only on the basis of a pre-conceived notion that they do not have the capacity to understand the complexity of a situation.

Manu's Views on Suggestions

Quite a similar advice comes from Manu, who has said:

विषादप्यमृतं ग्राह्यं बालादपि सुभाषितम्।
अमित्रादपि सदवृत्तम मेधादपि कांचनम्।।

(Viśādapyamṛtaṁ grāhyaṁ bālādapi subhāṣitam
Amitrādapi sadvṛttam medhādapi kāncanam)

— *Manu Smriti (2-214)*

Nectar should be extracted even from the poison, good suggestions of even a child should be accepted; good conduct should be learnt even from an enemy and gold be picked up even from the dirt.

Manu has gone a step further that not only the good ideas of children be accepted but the fair conduct should be learnt even from an opponent; such democratic advice is evidently opposed to authoritarianism. Consideration to the workers' suggestion is a great motivating factor and a morale booster too. The concept of Joint Management Councils carries this philosophy and has shown encouraging results.

Constitution of India

The philosophy of considering the suggestions of the workers as depicted in Indian scriptures has been the forerunner of the modern ideas. The 42nd Amendment of the Constitution in 1976 inserted a new Article 43 A that provides for participation of workers in the management. Even prior to this amendment, steps had been taken through non-statutory measures to secure such participation, in the shape of Joint Management Councils. The suggested scheme discussed above finds a prominent place in the councils. Further, the concept of Quality Circles is also based on the idea of participation of workers in the management of industries.

Conclusion

If the industry has to prosper in a country, there have to be continuous efforts made by the state, management managers and workers as well to develop the team spirit. The most suitable way to realise such goal is to cultivate and develop the human resource, as that constitutes the most important resource amongst all. Workers whose dignity has been properly taken care of, who find their place in the industry, whose morale has been high, and who are motivated to be loyal and sincere towards their goal become performers and lead to prosperity of the society and the nation. Managers are, thus, saddled with the great responsibility of cultivating their workforce.

ꝏ

4

Management by Example

Emergence of the Theory

A number of management theories have been evolved and practised during the 19th and 20th centuries. Some of them have won wide acclaim. Nevertheless, all managers or most of them have not adopted all the theories in their totality. The managers usually tend to adopt the theory most suited to their organisation in view of their workforce, situation, environment, organisation culture, their own calibre and so on. The theories, polices and strategies they adopt are either a mix of many others or are their own brainchild.

Considering all the policies and practices, one point emerges which is common to most of them and is always appreciated by the workforce, and that is the manager must act as a role model for his people. This can be termed as 'Management by Example'. This theory has the support of two natural tendencies — 'trees dry from the top' and 'percolation is from up to down'. A famous saying goes, 'practice is better than precepts'.

The most accepted truth in management is that any establishment shall be as good or bad as the managers want it to be. The managers have to set an example for the subordinates to emulate. The subordinates mostly behave like children who emulate their parents. The manager is their ideal person. If the manager in punctual, which they perceive, they follow the suit.

'An Example'

Taking a live example, the General Manager of an establishment noticed most officers and workers reporting late for the work. He neither issued any notice or circular nor issued any warning. All that he did was to come to the main gate fifteen minutes before the scheduled time and sit there, reading a book. In a week's time, the magic worked. Everyone started reporting for work on time.

The Theory

Theory of management by example has been an ancient practice, but is equally modern. The head person in a family manages the household. The family members go the way their head person goes. This head person is the role model for the children. The case with an organisation is similar to that with a family. Grafting and developing this policy suitably into the modern management system may work wonders.

The Indian scriptures, like *Srimad Bhagvat Gita*, *Mahabharata*, *Śukra Nitih*, Kautilya's *Artha Śastra* and others, have acclaimed this management theory. *Srimad Bhagvat Gita* says:

> यद् यद् आचरति श्रेष्ठः तद तदेवेतरो जनः ।
> स यत्प्रमाणं कुरुते लोकस्तदनु वर्तते ।।
> (Yad yad ācārati śresthaḥ tad tadevetaro janah
> sa yatpramānam kurute lokastadanu vartate)
>
> — *Srimad Bhagvat Gita (3-21)*
>
> *As the elite do, common people behave the same way. Whatever examples and standards are set by them (the elite) the people in general emulate the same.*

So far as this aspect is concerned, *Srimad Bhagvat Gita* may be seen surviving even today. Mahatma Gandhi adopted the practice of fasting (अनशन – Anśana) to purify his soul when he pressed some demand of national interest. The same practice still continues widely but in a distorted form in the name of 'hunger strike'. Anybody is now free to adopt this Gandhian method.

Common people emulate not only the deeds of great men but also their ways of life, and even clothes, Examples are the 'Gandhi Cap', 'Nehru Jacket', 'Rajiv Shawl', 'VP Singh Cap' and the like.

Sukra's Views

If a manager wants his subordinates to function in a particular manner, he must show the way by practising the same himself. If the subordinates are required to act promptly, the manager ought to make his promptness visible. Contributing to this thought, Śukra says:

स्वकार्ये शिथिलो यः स्यात किमन्ये न भवन्ति हि।
जागरूकः स्वकार्ये यस्तसाहयश्च तत्समाः ।।

(Svakārye śithilo yah syāt kimanye na bhavanti hi
jāgrükah svakārye yast tsahāyāsca tat samāḥ)

— *Śukra Nitih (4-2-35)*

One who is slack in his work, his subordinates also remain slack. One who himself is active in his work, his helpers too remain active and vigilant.

The truth inherent in the above statement cannot be learnt from the words alone. It is to be practised. If the boss is seen gossiping during the work time, it may be futile for him to expect his helpers to be working. When performers in a workforce see their manager working hard, they also follow the suit. When the boss works shoulder-to-shoulder with his people, their morale goes high, they tend to become star performers and try to contribute to the best of their abilities.

Kautilya's Views

The above thought has been reinforced by Kautilya. He says:

राजानमुत्थित मनूत्तिष्ठन्ते भृत्याः ।
प्रमाघन्तमनु प्रमाघन्ति ।।
कर्माणि चास्य भक्षयन्ति ।।

(Rājānmutthit manuthiṣthante bhrityāḥ
Pramadyantmanu pramādyanti
Karmāni cāsya bhakṣyanti)

When the king (substitute it with the manager or administrator) is active, the employees also become active following his example. If he is not active, then the employees also become negligent, slack and spoil the work.

Thus, Kautilya says that in order to make the subordinates active, the manager himself has got to be active. The helpers of a slack manager spoil the work. Thus, the manager's performance percolates downwards to his subordinates and workers.

The Other View

A famous saying is 'as you sow so shall you reap'. Based on a similar thought, Śukra says:

> सुपुण्यो यत्र नृपतिर्धर्मिष्ठास्तत्र हि प्रजाः ।
> महापापी यत्र राजा तत्राधर्मपरो जनः ।।
> (Supunyo yatra nripatirdharmiṣthāstatra hi prajāh
> Mahāpāpi yatra rājā tatrādharmaparo janah)
>
> — *Śukra Nitih (4-1-60)*

If the King is pious and dutiful, the people will also be the same. Where the King is sinful, there people also remain involved in sinister activities. (Substitute manager or leader for the king and workers for the people or praja; the couplet applies to industrial management).

If the manager is a pious one, the subordinates tend to be dutiful, the foremost reason being that the subordinates emulate their leader. Based on this principle, it has been said:

> यस्याश्रितो भवेल्लोकस्तद्वदाचरित प्रजा ।
> (Yasyàshrito bhavellokastadvadàcarit praja)
>
> — *Śukra Nitih (4-3-4)*

The way the patron lives his own life, the people start living the same way.

Though the statement relates to the King and his people or *praja*, it has much relevance to the industrial organisations. If the manager is active in his work, the subordinates (workforce) are also work-oriented.

Team Leader

No manager can produce results on his own, unless his team works in cohesion, with each member merging the excellence in his sphere with the objective of the team. When the team wins, all the members win, not the leader alone. The leader has to take proper care of appropriate placement of the members and also that their morale is high and it is constantly boosted up.

Team succeeds when the team leader acts as a binding force, and when the team members have full faith in the leader. This can be possible only when the leader portrays himself as a model for all the members of the team.

The leader ought to be followed with all sincerity is the crux of the Sanskrit saying:

महाजनो येन गता स पंथा ।

(Mahajano ye na gata sa panthah)

The way the great people go is the real and right path.

The saying given above being true, the responsibility then lies on the great ones to show the right path. They are burdened with the obligation to display what a fair conduct is, not by preaching sermons but by becoming a living example themselves.

Manager to Set Examples

The problem therefore comes up about the way the leader should behave so as to become active and capable of setting examples and becoming a model for the followers. The solution has been provided thus:

आत्मनश्च प्रजायाश्च दोषदर्श्युत्तमो नृपः ।
विनियच्छति चात्मानमादौ भृत्यांस्ततः प्रजाः ।।

(Ātamanaśca prajāyāśca doṣdarśyuttamo nṛpah
Viniyacchati cātmānmādou brityānstatah prajāh)

— *Śukra Nitih (4-1-76)*

The King (leader or manager) who looks after his own shortcomings and also those of his subordinates is adjudged to be good. He, thus, first gets rid of his own deficiencies and then helps his subordinates to get rid of them.

Know Self and the People

Thus, Śukra has given a useful formula that the manager's first obligation is self-analysis — know his own self. The injunction, therefore is 'Know thyself '. Unless one knows his own self and does not win over his own shortcomings, he cannot understand others and inspire them to reform themselves. Therefore, knowing one's own self is the key to knowing others.

A manager's other obligation is 'Know your people'. This can be possible only when one fulfils the earlier obligation of knowing his own self. When the leader knows his people, he becomes more effective as he knows how to deal with each one. Modern management thought is that the leader or the manager ought to know his people just as the mother knows her children. She understands who will work by advice, who by reprimand and who by twisting the ears and so on. The leader or manager possessing such knowledge about his people can adopt suitable strategies to get them going.

However, knowing and understanding one's own self is quite a tough task. The whole effort has to start from the top and go downwards, as per law of gravity. This thought, in a way is the forerunner of the modern concept of Johari Window (discussed in the next chapter). Self-perception or the area known to one's own self and also to others needs to be thoroughly analysed in the first instance. Then comes the area not known to self but known to others. This can be identified by proper appreciation of the feedback. If these two areas are properly appreciated and understood in the correct perspective, much can be possible in building effective relationships.

The thought as the *prima facie* appears to be simple but is hard to practise. It requires constant efforts to act accordingly. However, once the process begins, the rest is simple. In a celebrated couplet, the famous poet Kabir has said that when he started looking for a bad person he found none else than his own self. So the wisdom requires self-analysis and liberating one's own self from the shortcomings, followed by looking into others and defuse their deficiencies.

Army Leadership

The key to success of Indian Army is that the officers on top lead their men from the front and not at the back. When the officer orders 'attack!', he is seen in the front and is the first to attack. This is the highest morale booster. The industrial managers can also act in a similar way. If the manager is seen at various places of work, taking interest in the problems and progress, the workers get much encouraged.

The concept, 'Management by Example' is not of modern origin. Thinkers of the early period have deliberated upon this concept. However, it has not been accorded the pride of place that it deserves.

Perception about the Manager

No theory of management can succeed without close cooperation and understanding between the manager and his team. It is equally true that any theory of management may not succeed if the person to practise it does not perceive its benefits. One may adopt a policy with all faith and understanding about it, but it may hardly succeed unless the subordinates perceive the manager efficient enough to be emulated. Such effectiveness may develop when the manager has a clear perception of his own self and also that of his people as prescribed by Śukra.

Conclusion

The fact remains that the concept 'Management by Example' is one of the most effective methods of management. The method may suit most organisations, if not all. The key to success of this theory is in the safe hands of the managers if they so realise.

OO

5

Manager as a Leader

Manager as Leader

Manager leads his people towards the goal. He is the person who can get his people to follow him. He is the one who is looked up to, whose judgement is trusted, who inspires and warms the hearts of those working with him and for him and the one who knows how to explain his people what is needed to be done. His battle is for the hearts and minds of his people. He ought to have the capacity and the will to rally his workforce to a common purpose and the character that may inspire confidence.

Leader Born or Made

Leadership requires a close study of human nature. It is the people who are the factors of importance. Christ once said, "I will make you fishers of men." What Christ meant was that he would teach and train his disciples how to win the hearts of men. This implies that leadership has to be taught. Some are of the view that leaders cannot be made by teaching or training. However, the midway is more appealing. There are some who have within themselves the instincts and qualities of leadership in greater degree than others do. There are still some who have no characteristics of leadership. It is the former ones who can be developed as leaders by training.

Field-marshal Viscount Montgomery narrates his own case, "By the training, I had received from my superiors in peace time, I gained confidence in my ability to deal with any situation likely to confront a young officer of my rank in war; this increased my morale and my powers of leading my platoon, and later my company".

The greatest of all leaders, Krishna, had the patience and the calibre to narrate the whole *Srimad Bhagvat Gita* with 18 chapters and

700 *ślokas* to carve out the mightiest warrior of Arjuna who had refused to fight in any case. He patiently clarified the doubts that Arjuna placed before him, one after the other. Eventually, he emerged victorious in the battle of heart and mind.

Therefore, the concept that leaders are made rather than born is more close to truth — exceptions apart — still there is another category of those on whom leadership is thrust upon. Even such leaders have to develop themselves to be successful and effective. There again, training holds its importance.

Understand the People

Human relationship attains the top priority for a leader for the obvious reason that he leads people. Workforce is the basic requirement for any business. It is the people that the leader (manager) has to understand. A successful leader must develop a proper appreciation of human nature. He must enjoy the confidence of those whom he leads. Once such confidence is obtained, the leader has to explain the task and targets and how that can be accomplished. The subordinates are also to be enlightened about their position in the totality and also the impact of their success or failure on the ultimate goal. Finally, they have to be given a go-ahead along with the *modus operandi* of the action plan. Then, if the target or the goal is achieved, that is the success of the work team and not solely that of the leader. Apart from handling the work situation, the manager has to do the required morale boosting as well. He ought to be in touch with his people and show adequate interest in their personal problems. His people must perceive that their leader is the real guardian of their interests. Yet all this has to be done maintaining a respectable distance from the people. This concept of distance, the leader must appreciate and understand or else possibilities are there that the people may start taking liberties and the discipline may be in jeopardy.

Leadership Qualities

Thus, taking an overall view, the manager ought to be a dynamic person who may be capable of turning the adversities in his favour and to his gain. What then are the qualities that he should possess?

Much has been deliberated upon the qualities that a leader should possess by the thinkers of the West. What East has contributed on this issue also arouses interest. Indian thinkers and sages have also dealt with the subject. Yet, before dwelling on that subject, it needs to be brought out that Sanskrit equivalent of leader is *Neta* or *Nayak* which has been derived from *'Ni' dhatu* (root or source). The meaning of *'Ni' dhatu* (root) is to bring or get something, in this case the accomplishment of the target.

Prajapati as a Leader

Dealing with the duties of a Prajapati who heads the Nation, the *Rig Veda* says:

इन्दुरिन्द्रो वृषाः हरिः पवमानः प्रजापतिः ।
(Indurindro vrişā hariḥ pàvmānah prajāpatiḥ)

— *Rig Veda (9-5-9)*

*The person engaged in rearing, bringing up, cultivating and taking care of the people ought to be possessed of six qualities, '**Vrisa**' — should be strong, '**Indrah**' — must possess affluence and strength as to be able to destroy the enemy, '**Harih**' — remove the pains and agonies of his people, '**Pavamanah**' — be pious himself and make the people pious, '**Induh**' — give peace and happiness to the people, '**Prajapatih**' — be the rearer and preserver of the people, making them fearless and joyful.*

The leader should be a preserver and protector of the rights of the people. He ought to adopt such ways and means that the common man (people) may freely and fearlessly undertake their tasks.

Other Qualities

Describing the qualities of leader, the *Rig Veda* further says:

अच्छागिरो मतयो देवयन्तीरग्निं यन्ति द्रविणं भिक्षमाणाः ।
सुसंदृशं सुप्रतीकं स्वन्चं हव्यंवाहमरतिं मानुषाणाम् । ।
(Acchāgiro matayo devayantiragniḿ yanti
dravinaḿ bhikşamānāḥ
susandriśaḿ supratikaḿ svancaṃ
havyavāhamratiḿ mānuşāṇāḿ)

— *Rig Veda (7-10-3)*

The leader should be good and attractive to look at.

The above Vedic *richa* (a Vedic couplet) says that the person should possess an attractive and pleasing personality. He should have heart-winning and progressive manners and the capability of leading the people towards progress and betterment. Such leader has angel-like qualities; therefore the people who want to lead a godly life always follow such a leader and keep living a pious life. Living the godly way, in essence, means attainment of knowledge from the scholars and those who are knowledgeable. Information does not mean knowledge, which is much higher than the former. Often knowledge is lost in information. So, the persons who lead a higher kind of life are constantly in pursuit of knowledge. This is a leadership quality.

Further elaborating the leadership qualities, two Vedas say:

नृणां नर्यो नृतम।

(Nrinam naryo nritaṁ)

A good (effective and successful) leader acts for the benefits, betterment, welfare and upliftment of the people.

He/she dedicates his whole life for this mission and is considered a mighty and superior person who does everything he can for the upliftment of the people and the society. Thus, in essence, the Vedas lay great emphasis that the leader must be very attentive and active in ensuring the welfare, progress, well-being and happiness of the people and ultimately take care of the social good. Besides, he also has to be strong, having pleasing inward and outward personality and a host of other qualities.

Apart from the Vedas, the qualities of a leader or *Neta* have been dealt by other Indian scholars and sages. Bharat (the sage who composed *Nātya Śastra*) has said that the *Neta* is the person who leads his people towards the attainment of goal, despite all constrains (difficulties and struggle).

Bharat's Views on Qualities

Dealing with an important quality of leadership, Bharat said:

व्यसनी प्राप्य दुः खं वा युज्यतेभ्युदयेन यः ।
तथा पुरूषमाहुस्तं प्रधानं नायकं बुधाः ।।

(Vysani prāpya duḥkhaṁ vā yujyateabhudyen yah
Tathā puruṣamāhustaṁ pradhānaṁ nāyakaṁ budhāḥ)

— *Natya Śastra (24-21, 22)*

A wise leader is well-versed in his profession. He excels in everything he undertakes. Likewise in progressing and in the matter of going from heights to heights, he is ahead of all who are with him.

He is the one who identifies himself with the social well-being and prospers that way. Thus, Bharat places the leader above all, working with him. Whatever he does, he does in the best possible manner that others with him cannot. In the process, he climbs the ladders of progress and keeps the welfare of his people and the society, to be the supreme.

Analysing the thoughts of Bharat, it emerges that social well-being is the *Dharma* of the leader. *Atharva Veda*, defining *Dharma* says, *"Yato abhyudaya nishreyas siddhih sa dhamah"*, which means, higher thoughts, emotions and goal that lead to social upliftment is the ultimate *Dharma*. Therefore, social upliftment is of supreme importance and as such everything must ensure the social good. The leader ought to adopt ways and means to be successful and effective, but all his efforts must keep full consideration of the welfare of the society.

About the qualities that a leader ought to have, Bharat further elaborates that generally a leader should be polite, charming in speech and behaviour, unselfish, liberal, wise, soft spoken, popular, upright, pious, eloquent speaker, cultured, resolute, intelligent, zealous, of sharp memory, skilled in arts, self-respecting, brave, mighty, vigorous, familiar with codes, just observer of law and a torchbearer of social upliftment.

Dhananjaya's Views on Qualities

Taking a cue from the above qualities narrated by Bharat, it appears that about more than a thousand years later, Dhananjaya, a famous sage, in his treatise *Dasharoopaka*, wrote two couplets dealing with leadership qualities, which are:

नेता विनीतो मधुरस्य त्यागी दक्षः प्रियंवदः ।
रक्तलोकः शुचिर्वाग्मी रूढवंशः स्थिरो युवा ।।
बुध्युत्साहस्मृतिप्रज्ञ कलामान समन्वितः ।
शूरोदृढश्च तेजस्वी शास्त्रचक्षुश्च धार्मिकः ।।

(Netā vinīto madhurasya tyāgi dakshḥ priyaṁvadaḥ
Raktalokah śucirvāgmi rudhavamśaḥ sthiro yu vā
Budhyutsāhsmritipragya kalāmān samnvitaḥ
Śuro dridhaśca tejasvi sāstrocakşusca dhārmikah)

The qualities of a leader, as described in *Dasharoopaka* by Dhananjaya are just the same as those enumerated by Bharat, which were so exhaustive that the later writer could not add anything to them.

However a contemporary work, *Sahitya Darpan* went a step further to describe each quality one by one separately. The qualities have also been discussed in detail in that book thus:

शोभा विलासो माधुर्यं गांभीर्यं धैर्य तेजसी ।
लालित्यौदार्यं मित्यष्टौ सत्त्वजाः पौरुषा गुणाः ।।
(Śobhā vilāso mādhurayamं gāmभbhiryamं dharya tejasī
lālityaodāryamं mityasatau sattvajāḥ paurasāgunāḥ)

— *Sahitya Darpan (3-50)*

The leader according to the above couplet should have a charming inward and outward personality. Under this heading come, bravery, wisdom, truthfulness, zeal, love and affection, pity, mercy and respect for elders.

Under *vilas* come, compassionate looks, elegance in gait and smiling countenance. *Madhuryam* means in the face of a situation of acute tension, the leader must be able to keep his calm. *Gambhirya* means absence of tension, in spite of all its causative factors, like fear, grief, anger, joy. If in the face of such factors, the leader remains unmoved and maintains his poise, he has the quality of *gambhirya*. *Dhairya* is the patience in the face of adversities. *Tej* denotes the quality to retaliate when the leader may not be able to tolerate the insult and humiliation. *Lalitya* is the expressions of love and compassion. *Audaryam* includes generosity, help and protection to others, being soft spoken and protector and preserver of arts. These are the eight pious qualities that a leader ought to posses.

Sukra's Views on Qualities

Deliberating upon the qualities of a great leader, Śukra has said:

स्वदुर्गुणश्रवणतो यस्तुष्यति न क्रुधयति ।
स्वोपहासप्रविज्ञाने यतते त्यजति श्रुते ।।
स्वगुणश्रवणान्नित्यं समस्तिष्ठति नाधिकः ।
दुर्गुणानां खनिरहं गुणाधान कथं मयि ।।
मय्येव चाज्ञताऽप्यास्ति मन्यते सोऽधिकोऽखिलात ।।
(Svadurgunsravanato yastuṣati na krudhyati
Svopahāsapravijňāne yatate tyajyati shrute
Svagunaśvnānnityam samastisṭhati nādhikah
Durgunānām khanirahamं gunādhān kathamं mayi
Mayyeva cajňtapyāsti manyate sodhikokhilāt)

— *Śukra Nitih (3-307, 308)*

The person who is satisfied by listening to his/her shortcomings and does not get annoyed but tries to know more of them from the critics and gets rid of those deficiencies, who does not become over joyous on listening to his praise but maintains calm and thinks that he has the responsibility of being more and more elevated as compared to others is a wise person. It is such person who leads others. The common people emulate such enlightened ones.

Johari Window Concept

The thought propounded in the given couplet provides guidelines to the concept of 'Johari Window' developed by Luft and Ingham. Johari window is used to depict leadership personality. The leadership personality includes self-perception and the perception of others. There are behaviours and attitudes of the leader, which he indulges in and knows about them. These fall within the category 'Known-to-self' — 'self perception'. There are other areas that the leader is unaware of how they are coming across to others. These will depend upon the feedback and are called 'unknown to self' — 'perception of others'.

People should be allowed to have the feeling they want. Such feelings ought to be heard and accepted. People strongly cherish their feelings and perceptions. Therefore, the managers should never tell the people, "It is not your real feeling" or "That is not correct". Śukra has expressed a clear view about the opinions of critics, their usefulness as feedback, which the leader should consider, analyse and correct his behaviour, if need be. The leader must make effective arrangement for obtaining the necessary feedback.

Only One Leader

Managements of industrial organisations must make suitable arrangements to ensure that no person should be placed in the situation of dual leadership. One ought to have one leader who knows him and whom he knows. In this context, Śukra has said:

भात्येकनायकं नित्यं नैव निर्बहुनायकम् । ।

(Bhātyek nāyakaṁ nityaṁ naiva nirbahunāyakam)

— *Śukra Nitih (3-241)*

Till there is one leader, the organisation remains healthy.

If there are numerous leaders, the organisation gets spoilt. This is becoming a common dilemma faced by the managements. There are the rules in the organisation that lay down that the employee will approach higher authority, through a proper channel. Prudence demands that the same process be adopted at the higher levels, which rarely happens. The higher authority feels that they can always command anyone in the lower ranks. It is such practice that spoils the whole culture of the organisation and takes the form of indiscipline. It was Śukra's sagacious thought that even such details have been dealt in such early stage in the past.

Modern Thinkers Views on Qualities

Modern thinkers have also laid down the leadership qualities. Such qualities fall within the ambit of what the scriptures say; yet it may be of interest to enumerate them. The leader must have the capacity to concentrate and focus attention on the goal and the problem incidental to attain the same.

The leader must have an aptitude to take timely decisions. He ought to be sincere in his dealings. His attitude must be firm, fair, unshaken and consistent. He must be faithful and loyal towards his mission and the people. He must keep himself updated with the latest thought and behavioural technology. He must have a fair knowledge of his job and profession. Above all, a successful and effective leader must enjoy complete confidence of the people whom he leads.

Successful versus Effective Leadership

Leadership may be successful or effective or both. In this context, one may proceed with the basic assumption that when one attempts to affect the behaviour of another, this is called 'Attempted Leadership'.

- Leader's style may not be compatible, but the follower does the job because of the leader's position or power — this is successful leadership but not effective.
- The followers may do the job willingly to cooperate because the leader's request satisfies the follower's needs or goal — this is effective leadership.
- A successful leader emphasises upon position, power and close supervision.

- An effective leader depends on personal power and general supervision.
- A successful and effective leader depends on both, that is, the position, power as well as personal power.

Exercise of both the aforesaid powers needs a caution. Both the powers need to be appropriately and relevantly blended. Any laxity is likely to create the problems of indiscipline.

Conclusion

Study of leadership assumes higher priority in human resource management area. Basically, there are two reasons. One is that the manager is the leader of the people who work with him. Managers may well be called the captains of the industry. They have to lead the team from the front, rear and at all situations. The workforce gets inspiration from the managers and follows their examples. The other reason is that that any team, be it a play team or a work team, always needs a leader. This leader is the person who plans the tasks, guides the team and attains the goal. It is the team that succeeds. The leader is the first amongst equals. He knows the strengths and weaknesses of all the team members. He then has to supplement and complement each one of them. The leader is the person who infuses the team spirit amongst the members. Therefore, the leader has to be constantly alive to his responsibilities, which will be possible only when he understands and appreciates his role as a leader.

6

Managing by Least Supervision

Experiments and experiences of management thinkers and practitioners have shown that there are situations where the workforce prefers to work unsupervised, or least supervised. They tend to feel frustrated and demoralised, if controlled and directed at every step. They want to be their own supervisors and controllers. All they need is the help of experts. These are self-respecting, disciplined, responsible, wise and performing people.

The Seed

Such results indicate that dormant seeds exist and they sprout up in conducive climate and are nurtured by suitable care. It may be of interest to know where these seeds come from.

At times, a period or a situation comes in society when the people are knowledgeable, wise, disciplined and dutiful. Such people are self-governed. They do not need an administrator. However, as the society advances, and the situation so arises, the people create their own administrator who first coordinates and then administers.

Such was the time and situation in India during the Vedic period and later thereafter too. Similar stage and time has been seen in India many a times as the history tells us. It occurs and reoccurs from time to time. Commencing with the invasion of Alexander, the values were caught in the process of dilution. During the period of Chandragupta Maurya also, some organisations existed as replica of the old. Thereafter, the seeds became dormant, though they have shown up here and there, sparingly alone. Some instances of this age-old system are visible even today. The great example is that of an engineering organisation in Mumbai, which is functioning on these very principles. Then arises the question as to what this system of Vedic period was all about.

The Vedic System

This is known as the Prajapati system of state administration. In this form of administration, the people or the *praja* possessed the supreme rights of appointing the Prajapati. In the event of the Prajapati not acting as per the established norms, the people could remove him and appoint another person in his place. The straight argument favouring such supreme power was that the people could exist without a Prajapati, who in turn could not exist without the people.

The people or the *praja* used to exercise such supreme rights through their representatives in the two institutions called, the *'Gramsabha'* and the *'Rastra Samiti'*, commonly called the *'Sabha'* and the *'Samiti'*. They were known as the daughters of the Prajapati. The *Atharva Veda* says:

> सभा च मा समितिश्चावतां प्रजापतेर्दुहितरो संविदाने।
> येना संगच्छा उप मास शिक्षाच्चारुवदानि पितरः संगतेषु।।
> (Sabhā ca mā samiścāvatāṁ prājpaterduhitaro samvidāne
> yenā samgacchā up mās śikşāccaāru vadāni pitaraḥ smgateşu)
>
> — *Atharva Veda (7-13-1)*

'Gramsabha' and 'Rashtra Samiti' are the two daughters of 'Prajapati'. They impart true knowledge to the administrator, and can also protect him. O! Ancestor like members, the one (member) whom I contact may suggest and explain the matters of national interest. I (Prajapati) shall speak well and beneficently in the 'Samiti' and 'Sabha'.

The Prajapati was bound in duty to protect the *Gramsabhas* and *Rashtra Samiti* who in turn patronised the Prajapati. The *sabhas* and the *samiti* guided and advised the Prajapati in day-to-day administration.

Every village was to have a *sabha* comprising the members elected by the village people. The *sabhas* were to look after all the affairs of the village such as the protection and safety, education, dispensing of justice and health etc. Such *sabhas* were also to elect the members of the *Rashtra Samiti*, which was to undertake administration with Prajapati as its head. The *samiti* was also obliged to elect the Cabinet Ministers.

It was the *Rashtra Samiti's* right to elect the Prajapati. In this manner, right from the *Gramsabha* to the Prajapati, all were elected by the people. Such was the sagacity, responsible charter, discipline and patriotism prevailing amongst the people in such remote past.

Qualities of a Prajapati

In the context of the qualities that Prajapati should possess, the *Atharva Veda* lays down:

धाता मित्रः प्रजापतिः ।
(Dhata mitrah Prajapatih)

— Atharva Veda (11-9-25)

Prajapati is the saviour and protector of people.

शं प्रजापतिः ।
(Śm Prajapathih)

— Atharva Veda (19-9-6)

May the Prajapati maintain peace and on that the evil may not be able to spread!

अश्विनोभा प्रजापतिः प्रजयावर्धयन्तु ।
(Aśvinobhā Prajāpatih prajayā vardhayantu)

— Atharva Veda (14-2-13)

With the help of the medical men, the Prajapati may undertake the welfare of the people. The Prajapati may protect and save the people from all evils and perpetuate them.

प्रजापतिर्निधिपतिर्नः ।
(Prajāpatirnidhipatirnaḥ)

— Atharva Veda (7-18-4)

May the Prajapati be the protector of our wealth and the Dharma!

सत्यधर्मा प्रजापतिः ।
(Satyadharmā Prajāpatih)

— Atharva Veda (7-24-1)

Prajapati should be the protector of Dharma!

प्रजापतिः निधिपा देवः ।

(Prajapatiḥ Nidhipā Devaḥ)

— Vạjsyèn Yajurved (8-17)

Prajapati should be physically and mentally strong. He should be the protector of the dignity, wealth and well-being of the people.

पवमानः प्रजापतिः ।

(Pavamanh Prajapatih)

— Rig Veda (9-5-9)

Prajapati should himself be pious and spread piety amongst all.

ब्रह्मचारी प्रजापतिः ।

(Brahmacari Prajapati)

— Atharva Veda (11-5-16)

Prajapati should be brahmachari, which means that he should have studied at the Gurukul. He should possess the divine qualities.

Based on the above qualities, the Prajapati should be an ideal person. He should have full consideration for the rights of the people vis-à-vis his own. He is bound in duty to uphold sanctity of the commonly accepted rules, customs, practices and social norms. He should be the protector and saviour of the people, their wealth and be keen on their all-round welfare. He should take care of the law and order and ensure maintenance of peace in the nation. Public health and complete development of the people should also be his concern. Besides, he must be a person of high moral standards and pious and unbiased character.

Functioning of Prajapati

In the modern period, the President of the country is a person whose functioning is not visible to the people. He is rarely visible to the common man. However, in the Vedic period the Prajapati was to function with openness. In this context, the *Atharva Veda* says:

प्रजापतिरेव तत् प्रजाभ्यः प्रादुर्भवति ।

प्रजापतेऽनु मा बुध्यस्व ।

अन्वेनं प्रजा अनु प्रजापतिर्बुध्यते ।।

(Prajāpatireva tat prajābhyaḥ prādurbhavati
Prajāpatenu mā budhysva
Anvenamí prajā anuprájāpatirbudhyate)

— *Atharva Veda (9-1-24)*

Prajapati, the protector and rearer of the people comes for their benefit. May he come out and function! He may look after the people and the people may reciprocate.

The Prajapati should come out and be delighted in the company of the people. The Prajapati and the officers may live together with sympathy and render mutual help to one another and prosper.

Prajapati to own the Nation's Land

...धता भुवनस्य प्रजापतिः ।

(Dhatā bhuvansya prājapātiḥ)

— *Atharva Veda (4-53-2)*

Prajapati owns the land.

The real intent is that the Prajapati owns all the land of the nation in his name and office as a custodian. Owning thus, he is bound in duty to protect the land from any enemy. He must do all in his might to develop and make the land more fertile. Execution of this policy was to be taken care of by the *sabha* and *samiti* but a specific policy was to be laid down and its implementation ensured.

Housing for the People

In this matter, it has been said:

प्रजायै चक्रे त्वा शाले परमेष्ठी प्रजापतिः ।

(Prajāyai cakre tvā śāle parmeṣathi prājāpatih)

— *Atharva Veda (9-3-11)*

Prajapati should construct houses for the people to live in.

This means that the responsibility for construction of the houses was that of the state, especially for such people who could not afford to construct their own houses. The saints, preachers, low-paid employees could not construct their own house, so they could live in the state-built houses. The whole purpose was that nobody should be left without a dwelling.

On Administration of Water Supply

The *Atharva Veda* says:

प्रजापतेर्वो धामान्स्मै लोकाय सादये।।

(Prajāpatervo dhāmnāsmai lokāya sādaye)

—*Atharva Veda (10-5-7-14)*

The water supply is being installed here on the basis of the orders of the Prajapati for the benefit of the people.

The intent and purpose was that the Prajapati, on the basis of the rules, ought to issue notification for acquiring the land for the water supply sources, like the wells, ponds, canals etc. Every citizen should have access to the source of water. The water supply should have wholesome drinking water.

Business and Trade Promotion

येन धनेन प्रपणं चरामि धनेन देवा धनमिच्छमानः ।
तन्मे भूयो भवतु मा कनीयोऽग्ने सातध्नो
देवान हविषा निषेध।।
तस्मिन् म इन्द्रो रुचिमदधातुप्रजापतिः सविता सोमो अग्निः ।।

(Yen dhanen prapanḿ carāmi dhanen devā dhanamicchamānaḥ
Tanme bhuyo bhavatu mā kanīyogne sātadhno devàn haviṣā niṣedha
Tasmin ma Indro rucimaddhātu prajāpatiḥ suvitā somo agniḥ)

—*Atharva Veda (3-15-5 & 6)*

Here the trading people pray that whatever capital I am investing for the trade and business with the purpose of earning more money may be sufficient and may not fall short of the requirement. O! Mighty one, please get such people away from me who reduce the profits, so that they may not be able to harm me. May God keep me interested in the trade and business pursued by me! May the Prajapati encourage those who are engaged in trade or business and keep away such person who harms the traders and businessmen! The trading community requests in a way that the prices may be maintained stable and the trade and commerce people may be given full protection and support by the state!

The concept is that in the national interest, there should exist workshops, factories and business houses and their setting up should be encouraged. This provides employment and generates more. It was considered the duty of the state to appoint more officers to inspect and ensure that proper facilities and encouragement was provided to let the trade and business grow and flourish. Protection against those who hinder the progress was considered equally important.

Food Grains to be made available to the People

In this matter, the *Atharva Veda* says:

यत्ते अन्नं भुवस्पत आक्षियति पृथिवीमनु।
तस्य नस्त्वं भुवस्पते सं प्रयच्छ प्रजापते।।
(Yatte annam bhuvaspate ākṣiyàti prithivimanu
Tasya nastvam bhuvaspate sam praccha Prājapate)

— Atharva Veda (10-5-45)

O! Rearer and conserver of the motherland and the people, give us all our share of the food grain available on our land.

This means that the distribution system should be so managed that the food grain that grows in the motherland should first be available for use of the people of the country. The system should not be such that the countrymen may live in deprivation and the food may be sent to other countries. This should never happen. The logic is that the child has the first and foremost right on the mother's milk.

Prajapati as a Treasurer of the Nation

उपोहश्च समूहश्च क्षत्तारौ ते प्रजापते।
ताविहा वहतां स्फातिं बहु भूमानमक्षितम।।
(Upohśca samuhśca kṣttaru te prājapate
Tavihā vahtāṁ sphātiṁ bahu bhumānmakṣitam)

— Atharva Veda (3-24-7)

This is addressed to Prajapati. O! Prajapati, those who earn and bring wealth and those who accumulate it, both are the treasurers. May the two bring in this land very large amounts that may never finish!

Here is the wish not only for those who earn wealth for the nation but also for those who preserve it and grow the national wealth. That means a desire to grow the national wealth to that extent that the same may not ever exhaust and keep growing from height to heights.

Dispenser of Justice

This is an important function for the Prajapati to act and ensure that everyone concerned act accordingly.

दृष्ट्वा रूपे व्याकरोत सत्यानृते प्रजापतिः ।
अश्रद्धामनृतेऽदधात् श्रद्धां सत्ये प्रजापतिः ।।
(Drişatvā rūpe vyākrot satyānrite prajāpatiḥ
Ashradhāmnriteadadhāt shradhāṁ satye Prājapatiḥ)

— *Vạjsyèn Yajurved (19-77)*

The Prajapati saw and examined both, the false and the true aspects and decided the issue. He did not rely on the falsehood, but appreciated and decided the truth, which means that he sided with the truth and opposed the falsehood and punished it.

Every case has two aspects, the false and the true. There is always a dispute between the two. Such disputes ought to be settled by the administrative machinery. The Prajapati appointed judges to administer justice on his behalf and sometimes on a matter of national importance, he himself undertook such responsibility.

On Miscellaneous Assignments

प्रजापतिर्विश्वकर्मा विमुंचतु ।
(Prajāpatirviśvakarmā vimuncatu)

— *Vạjsyèn Yajurved (12-61)*

Prajapati who is the Vishvakarma should be able to undertake various functions for the welfare of the people. He should relieve the people from all sufferings and miseries.

The term 'Vishvakarma' means the one who can perform all the acts. The main responsibilities of the Prajapati were rearing, bringing up and protecting the people. Therefore, he ought to be able to perform all the functions connected with the said tasks, that is, rearing and protecting the people.

Performing all the tasks like the Vishavakarma is not easy, so the Prajapati had to be capable of tolerating and bearing all the pains involving all the functions.

The kind of Prajapati that the *praja* expects is clearly written in the couplet given below:

प्रजापतेः प्रजा अभूम ।
(Prajapateh praja abhum)

— *Vạjsyèn Yajurved (9-21, 18-29)*

We shall be the subjects (praja or people) of such a person who rears and brings up the people well and is always careful about watching their interest. The person who cannot watch the interest of the people will never be our ruler. Such an evil-doer shall never be tolerated.

The people (*praja*) always desire that they may enjoy all prosperity (वयं स्याम पतयो रयीणां — Vayaṁ syám patayo rayīnām). The people may have more and more sources of a comfortable life. It was with such aim that the state needed to be administered and managed. Such officers and executives were to be appointed for undertaking the said responsibilities, who were the fittest for the functions assigned to them.

मा: ते जुहुम: तत् न अस्तु।

(Maḥ te juhumah tat na astu)

The desires and the purposes for which we pay taxes, that happiness, comforts and peace may we get! We may be prosperous and enjoy life.

It was for such reasons that the state administration had to strive as the state had mainly come into being mainly for those reasons.

Prajapati System and Modern Man-management

A glimpse of the ancient system, as described in this chapter, has a lot to inspire the modern managers in the human resource area. Most managers have one or the other man-management problem. They constantly are in search for solutions. Most of them are eager for a cut-and-dried formula.

However, that is difficult for the reasons that wherever man is involved, generalisations become a rare possibility if not completely impossible. Moreover, the fast changes often jeopardise generalisation which might otherwise last for a reasonably longer period. The result is that each case needs to be dealt with its own merits.

We have almost arrived at a stage where the process of erosion of values has adopted serious dimensions. Frustration, demoralisation, indiscipline, irresponsibility, lack of commitment and sincerity, mutual distrust and hatred, inhuman behaviour and a host of evils are catching up the scene. Both, the employers and employees are their victims, indulging in accusing one another.

The state created a massive public sector in the hope to set up an ideal employer. However, experience has shown that the public sector, being close to the corridors of power, tend to become soulless entities.

Quoting Franklin D. Roosevelt, "Concentration of economic power in all embracing corporation represents private enterprise becoming a kind of a private government which is a power unto itself — a regimentation of other people's money and other people's lives".

The Indian Supreme Court has further observed, "A corporation is an artificial being, invisible, intangible and existing only in the contemplation of the law. Being a mere creature of the law, it possesses only those properties, which the charter of its creation confers on it, either expressly, or as incidental to its very existence. Those are such as are supposed best calculated to affect the object for which it was created. Among the most important are immortality, and if the expression be allowed, individuality, properties by which a perpetual succession of many persons are considered the same, and may act as a single individual."

The public sector could not emerge as a model employer but has inflicted a serious damage of polluting the industrial scene and also the employers in the private sector. Still the fact remains that there exist organisations in the private sector even today where the employer and employee work in harmony and dignity. Without naming the organisation, it is worth mentioning that an effort to nationalise that organisation was opposed tooth and nail not by the employers but by the employees.

During these sixty years after independence, various laws have been enacted covering almost all the industrial matters. The Constitution of India containing 395 Article in 22 parts, worded so that social justice appears to be its conscience and the state as a partner of economic justice. However, the social justice now appears to be long away. The employers, who are now being called the management, and the employees, still continue to look one another with suspicion. The attitudes have changed the initial harmony and amicability into distrust, hatred, long drawn litigations and exploitation. This was the natural result of extensive legislation that acted only as an inferior motivator. The obvious question that arises is what action could be taken by all concerned towards bringing about a positive change in the attitudes of the management, employees, the trade unions and the state machinery as well.

A questioning mind, packed with the images of the glorious past, wants to understand if it should also remain a passive onlooker. Because the high sounding expressions of the modern age will hardly make any effect! The solution lies in bringing about a positive change in the attitudes of all those who have any concern with the industry, such change of attitudes may appear to be a utopia which certainly it is not. It is a goal that is difficult to achieve, but not impossible. There is no reason why we may desist from forging ahead only because the goal is difficult. There are goals that may take many years, decades, even a century or generations to achieve, but if the efforts continue in the right direction, they are bound to be realised. Now the question arises, how to make a beginning?

How to Make a Beginning

Dissemination of Information — As the first step, we may spread the message about the Prajapati system of administration and management through lectures, workshops, seminars and other such programmes jointly for the management personnel and employees. This will make headway towards enlightening their vision and also pave the way for further action. Information about the system can further be disseminated through common training, orientation and reorientation programmes to be repeated time and again to cover everything and for further continuation of the same. The other step for spreading information may be to publish posters, leaflets, pamphlets etc, suggesting some highlights of the system. For example, there may be a poster to show that the workers are the co-owners of the industry. The poster may be carrying slogans, like "Let us make our organisation grow and flourish so that we may prosper" or "We work for this organisation and we belong to it", and so on.

Management Games — Such games of changing the roles on different issues may be developed which may be played on special occasions and in some picnics to be jointly organised.

Joint Exercises — Mass exercise involving everyone, from the Managing Director to the labour, may be organised. Such exercises may be done every day before the resumption of work.

Self-Sorting of Problems — Whenever a problem arises, the supervisor or manager may sit with the workers to find out a workable solution suited for the morale and dignity of both the parties.

Involve Everyone Concerned — In all matters of shop floor, the manager, supervisors and workers should all sit together to plan, fix targets, execute the plans and all the rest. All decisions may be so taken that they may appear to have been taken unanimously.

Management Information — Managers, supervisors and workers should be made aware about the corporate goal, the progress made, the bottlenecks and what is expected of the personnel at all levels vis-à-vis their position and place in the overall picture.

Education System — In the initial stages, suitable capsules be provided to enlighten the young ones on the matters connected with fellow-feeling and brotherhood. With the help of stories, they may be given lessons as:

आत्मनः प्रतिकूलानि परेषाम् न समाचरेत।

(Atmanah pratikūlani pareśām na samācharet)

Whatever is adverse to you, do not do the same unto others.

आत्मवत सर्वभूतेषु।

(Atmavat sarvabhūteśu)

Treat everyone as your own self.

Having such background, when the young ones grow up, they become the citizens of broad vision. Educational programmes of similar nature can be evolved for those involved in the industry. The above and similar or new methods, depending upon the region and the people, can be developed and implemented. These methods will bring about attitudinal changes, which can be followed by other steps in order to further the cause.

Interaction with Serving Personnel — The supervisors and managers are on different steps in the hierarchy, mostly in the ascending process. They always crave for success, for which they must be effective in their positions. A supervisor or manager can be as effective as he wants to be. He has to realise and understand that the index of success lies in quality production and man-management.

The production side too depends, to a large extent, on the manager's dealing with his team. So the human resource assumes the pride of place in the race for effectiveness. Any supervisor or manager ought to appreciate that the workers are the producers of goods; therefore, they are the real resource. This is one resource that has the potential to appreciate while others depreciate. The supervisors and the managers owe their existence to the workforce and not vice-versa. It is, therefore, essential that human resource must be developed to its capacity.

Care needs to be taken that workers take pride in their workmanship. They adopt a positive attitude towards the organisation, industry and the society. They may develop a feeling that their work is the nation building work and not only limited to earning their livelihood. They have to work in an atmosphere of fellow-feeling and brotherhood. If they want to maintain their self-respect, they must have respect for their peers and superiors. Any damage to the organisation's goods or property is their own damage.

Conclusion

Summing up, there is need for a drastic change in attitudes, behaviour, values and standards of all those who are engaged in industrial pursuits. The guidelines may be taken from the Prajapati system of administration and management, glimpses of which have been presented in this chapter. Even humble efforts in this direction would show encouraging results. The programmes are to be taken up in a modest way, as the results are likely to be visible after prolonged efforts and practice. It is a silent revolution to be undertaken with complete patience, not to be hurried about. The results will start showing up in due course of time. The progress may be slow but the goal can be attained for sure. Some day it will be realised that everyone in the industry shall be so responsible that the supervision shall be least needed yet the managers shall be there, as leaders of the work teams and experts.

OO

7

The Knack of Winning People

Winning People

Attracting and winning people, friend, foe or otherwise is an age-old skill. The art is mostly practised everywhere and many thinkers have elaborated upon this concept. However, on going to the roots, Indian thinkers are visible. Śukra, the guru of demons, has made rich contributions. He names four *upāyās* (strategies or tactics) namely, *Sam*, *Dan*, *Bhed* and *Dand*. These rules have been in practice since remote past. They have stood the test of time and have merged with the experience of a multitude of people. Yet they are fresh, ready to be tried by the present and future generations. However, the methods can be used effectively only after their clear implications are realised.

Efficacy of the Upāyās

Describing the efficacy of the four efforts, Śukra has said:

> मित्रं शत्रुं यथायोज्ञैः कुर्यात स्ववशवर्तिनम् ।
> उपायेन यथा व्यालो गजः सिंहोऽपिसाध्यते ।।
> (Mitraṁ shatruṁ yathayojñaiḥ kuryāt svavaśvartinam
> upāyen yathā vyālo gajaḥ sinhoapisādhyate)
>
> — *Śukra Nitih (4-1-24)*

As by the efforts, the snake, elephant and lions can be tamed, so by adopting appropriate measure (upāyā), a friend and even a foe can be won over.

Any strategy (*upāyā*) in itself can hardly be useful. It is a combination of the situation, the person, appropriateness and suitability of the strategy that makes it successful.

Order of Use of Strategies

The four strategies have been allotted an order, a hierarchy with definite purpose. In the context of the order in which these ought to be used, it has been laid down as:

सामैव प्रथमं श्रेष्ठं दानं तु तदनन्तरम् ।
सर्वदा भेदनं शत्रोर्दण्डनं प्राण संशये । ।

(Sāmaiva prathamaṁ śreṣtham dānaṁ tu tadnaṅtaram
Sarvadā bhedanaṁ śatraurdandanaṁ prān sanśaye)

— *Śukra Nitih (4-1-37)*

At first, use of the Sam strategy is beneficial. If, that does not serve the purpose, the other policy dan should be adopted. If that too fails to be effective, then bhed should be used in all its ways. With bhed strategy also remaining ineffective, dand should be used.

Such course of action has been prescribed mainly for an enemy. Yet this can be the usual practice; another suggestion that emerges is that adherence to the prescribed order is not necessarily to be followed strictly. The policies may vary according to the person, situation and contingency, etc. It appears that Śukra himself was aware of such a situation where it may not be practicable to use the strategies one after the other. He says:

कृया भेदादुपाया हि भिघन्ते च यथार्हतः ।
(Kriyā bhedādupāyā hi bhidynte ca yathārhatah)

— *Śukra Nitih (4-1-35)*

As per the needs of the situation, the person on whom these policies are to be used, and his status, the order for use of the four strategies may vary.

Appropriate Use

The four strategies are like medicines that are used in consideration of the ailment, its character, the patient, his age and response, the possible reactions and the like factors. For example, if a person responds favourably to the *bhed* policy, the *bhed* should be used solely and not others. This can be further reinforced by the other measures without going by the prescribed order strictly, the reason being that the purpose of the use of these strategies needs to be served. Śukra has said that the one conversant with the policies should use each one of them so that the people can be won over and the opponents may not become stronger than his own self. Yet, it may not be safe and appropriate to draw universal conclusions. The proper course of action would be 'to see as to what policy should be adopted in relation to a person'.

Śukra has gone to the extent of prescribing some cases and the appropriate policy that may be adopted. Those will be taken a little later, the reason being that correct implication of each strategy has to be clearly understood.

Sam to a Friend

The strategy of *sam*, in relation to a friend, has been described as:

त्वत्समस्तु सखा नास्ति मित्रे साम इदम् स्मृतम्।
(Tvatsamastu sakhā nāsti mitre sām idam smritam)

— *Śukra Nitih (4-1-36)*

To tell a friend, 'there is no other friend like you' is the appropriate sam strategy so far as a friend is concerned.

Appreciation of the friendly qualities tends to elevate the ego of the person and brings him closer and as such motivates him to behave like a true friend. Replication of such behaviour towards a friend may result in winning him over.

Sam to an Opponent

Regarding the use of the *sam* strategy to an enemy, Śukra says:

परस्परमनिष्टं न चिन्तनीयं त्वयामया।
सुसाहास्यं हि कर्तव्यं शत्रौ साम प्रकीर्तितम।।
(Parasparmaniṣtaṁ na cintniyam tvayā mayā
Susāhāsyaṁ hi kartvyam shatrau sām prakiŕtitam)

— *Śukra Nitih (4-1-28)*

You should not think of causing harm, rather we should help one another.

Saying so constitutes *ṣam* words for an enemy. This expression may help in winning over an enemy. On the other hand, the expression may create mutuality of interest and may also exalt the other person's ego, though the hidden purpose may be to bring round the enemy or to enlist his unconditional support. Mere use of such expression tends to produce favourable results.

The *sam* strategy aims at appeasing and pleasing a friend or friendly person, so that he remains in high spirit and may perceive the user of the strategy as the person who in the real sense is the guardian of his interest. The enemy or opponent against whom the *sam* tactics is used perceives a community of interest and fellow-feeling. The *sam* method is capable of winning over the friend and foe alike.

Dan to a Friend and Enemy

The second strategy for winning people is *dan*; it is described as:

मम सर्वतवै वास्ति दानं मित्रे सजीवितम् ।

(Mam sarvaṁtāvai vāsti dānaṁ mitre sajīvitam)

— *Śukra Nitih (4-1-28)*

Telling a friend that 'along with my life, all that I have is you' is dan expressed in words to a friend.

The *dan* strategy to an enemy can be expressed as:

करैर्वा प्रमीर्तिर्ग्रामैर्वत्सरै प्रबलं रिपुम् ।
तोषयेत्तद्धि दानं स्याद्यथायोग्येषु शत्रुषु । ।

(Karairvā pramirtirrgrāmairvatasre prabalaṁ ripum
Tośyettaddhi dānaṁ syādyathāyogyayeṣu śatruṣu)

— *Śukra Nitih (4-1-32)*

Giving some revenue, a small village or something else for a year to a strong enemy and thus appeasing him is called dan strategy towards an enemy.

The crux of *dan* strategy is gifting something or promising to gift it. Any of these courses can be adopted as per the need. Though the real form of gift requires nothing in return, yet a sufficiently large number of people resort to the *dan* strategy in expectation of some advantage.

Dan strategy is commonly used in the present political situation, both at national as well as international levels. Many countries grant aid to other countries either on a friendly basis or for political consideration.

The aids granted on friendly basis have lesser ties or conditions attached to the aid, while politically motivated ones attach several conditions to bind the country so that it may become dependent upon the loaning country. Thus, the *dan* policy is gainfully used.

Amongst individuals too, *dan* is much in practice. When one person tries to win over the other, gifts play a vital role. This measure in the form of help becomes more powerful as it easily fulfils the need of the other person and cements relationship as well. It is this *dan* strategy that is mostly used in modern times and has now been corrupted.

Bhed for a Friend and a Foe

The third strategy is *bhed*; like the earlier two measures, *bhedas* have also been defined separately for a friend and for a foe. For a friend, it has been said:

मित्रेन्य मित्र सुगुणान् कीर्तयेद भेदनं हि तत।
(Mitreanya mitra sugunan kirtayed bhedanam hitat)

— *Śukra Nitih (4-1-29)*

In the presence of a friend, praising another friend is the bhed effort, for a friend.

In the context of an enemy, the *bhed* measure is:

शत्रु साधक हीनत्व कारणात प्रवलाश्रयात्।
तद्धीनतोज्जीवनाच्च शत्रु भेदन मुच्यते।।
(Śatru sādhaka hīnatva kārnāt pravlāśrayāt
Taddīnatojjīvnācca śatru bhedan mucyate)

— *Śukra Nitih (4-1-33)*

To weaken the strong measure of the enemy, seeking shelter of a stronger one and to impart strength to all the weak ones opposed to the enemy constitute bhed measure towards an enemy.

The *bhed* strategy is more psychological in nature. Its purpose is to create doubt about the ability of the one against whom the measures *sam* and *dan* have failed. Such a person should be given a perception that if he does not cooperate, there are still others who would be ready to help, and in that case he/she may lose the relation already existing. Thus, the *bhed* tactic, in a way, compels the other person to cooperate.

In the *bhed* technique, the one using it has to find some black spot or loophole in the career or character of the person against whom the measure is to be used. The user so manipulates the affairs that the person develops a feeling that if he does not remain within the fold of the user of the measure, he will be in a serious trouble. It is thus that the person gets won over. While in *sam* and *dan* measures, there is no fear element; in *bhed*, fear operates strongly.

Dand for a Friend and a Foe

Ultimately, in the event of all the three measures *sam*, *dan* and *bhed* having failed, there yet remains a fourth and a very strong strategy known as *dand*, which has been described thus:

मित्रे दण्डो न करिष्ये मैत्रीमेवं विधोऽसि चेत् ।
(Mitre dando na karişye maitrimevaḿ vidhosi cet)

— *Śukra Nitih (4-1-29)*

If you are like this, I will not keep friendship with you. This, in words, is the expression of dand to a friend.

Further with regard to an enemy, it has been said:

दस्युभिः पीडनं शत्रौ कर्षणं धन धान्यतः ।
तच्छिद्रदर्शना दुग्र बलैर्नीत्या प्रभीषणम् ।।
प्राप्तयुद्धानिवृत्तित्वस्त्रसनं दण्ड उच्यते ।।
(Dasyubhiḥ pīdanaḿ śatrau karşnaḿ dhan dhānyataḥ
Tacchidradaŗśnā dugra balairnītyā prabhişnam
Prāptayuddhānvrittitvastrasanaḿ dand ucayate)

— *Śukra Nitih (4-1-34)*

Getting the enemy robbed by dacoits, destroying his wealth and his store of food grains, finding out his weaknesses and then frightening him with a strong army and aggressive policy, continuing the battle against him, terrorising him constitute dand strategy for the enemy.

The word *dand* conveys various meanings, such as punishment, administration, law, etc. In this context, it is punishment. When *sam*, *dan* and *bhed* strategies fail to be effective, *dand* is the last resort, the total compulsion.

Do Not Use Bhed or Dand on a Friend

Use of the *dand* strategy on a friend has not been considered proper, and so also the *bhed*. Śukra has said:

मित्रे च सामदानेन स्तो न कदा भेद दण्डेन।
(Mitre ca sāmdānen sto na kadā bhed danden)

— Śukra Nitih (4-1-39)

Only sam and dan measures are appropriate to be used on a friend. Bhed and dand should never be used against him.

Here Śukra has issued a few injunctions, which need to be considered and respected.

Restraint in Use of Dand

However, the enemy needs to be subjected to harsh punishment. Yet, it ought to be taken care that the purpose of *dand* is to win over the enemy, not to destroy him. Therefore, the doses of dand should be so regulated that its use must be stopped at the stage when its purpose is served. When the enemy gets cornered, he starts cooperating. Thus any excess in *dand* is futile and might produce adverse results. So the user of *dand* must know the limits.

The matter of limits of *dand* is relevant for the other reason that the ultimate control of the *dand* always remains with the user. Instead of crossing limits, the strategy can be used again if need be. That may be more effective than crossing the limits of its use!

Suitable Strategies for Enemies

The enemies too are of different types on the basis of their strength. Śukra, therefore, has suggested the strategies to be adopted in relation to the strength of the enemy in the shape of the *śloka* given below:

प्रबलेऽरौ सामदाने सामभेदोऽधिके स्मृतौ।
भेददण्डौ समे कार्यौ दण्ड पूज्यः प्रहीनके।।
(Prabalearau Sāmdāne sām bhedoadhike smṛtau
Bhed dandau same kāryaur dand pujyaḥ prahinke)

— Śukra Nitih (4-1-38)

Sam and dan should be used with very strong enemy, sam and bhed be used with the enemy stronger than the self, and bhed and dand with an enemy of equal strength, and only dand for a weak enemy.

The approach of Śukra is highly practical. He has prescribed the use of strategies, which can be practised commonly, yet there may be cases needing deviation.

Use of the Strategies by Managers

Though, Śukra has prescribed the use of the four strategies mostly in reference to Kings, but they can be gainfully used by one and all. For example, if a manager has to use some measure on his workforce, a cue may be taken from the prescription about the use of the measures by the King towards his people (*praja*), where the teacher has said:

स्वप्रजानां न भेदेन नैव दण्डेन पालनम् ।
कुर्वीत सामदानाभ्यां सर्वदा यत्नमास्थितः ।।
(Svaprajānām̐ na bheden naiva danden pālnam
Kurvita sāmdānābhyām̐ sarvadā yatnamāsthitaḥ)

— *Śukra Nitih (4-1-41)*

Treat your people carefully with sam and dan, not by bhed or dand.

This injunction is based mainly on human relation. *Sam* and *dan* strategies constitute positive approach. Appreciate your people, give incentives and motivate them. Such approaches work well. On the other hand, *bhed* and *dand* being negative measures create differences among the team and their confidence is shaken, which is counter-productive.

Care of Opponents

Even the people harassed by the opponent need to be cultivated as the measure suggested by the following *śloka*:

रिपुप्रपीडितानां च साम्ना दानेन संग्रहः ।
(Ripuprapiditanam ca samna danen sangrah)

— *Śukra Nitih (4-1-40)*

People harassed and hurt by the opponent should be preserved and supported with the help of sam and dan measures.

This again is wisdom for the managers. There are always some people who are opposed to the manager; if they are not cared for, they might team up with the opponents because of which the number of opponents would swell manifolds. However if such people are won over by *bhed* and *dand* measures, the opponent gets weaker and may be compelled to come within the fold. Therefore, the wise policy calls for appeasement and motivation of those who have been at one time or the other been harassed by the opponent. This can be accomplished by the use of *sam* and *dan* measures, and that is what Śukra pleads as this is a practical and time-tested method of winning people.

Dand to be Well Considered

Śukra, then, deals with the appropriateness of the *dand* measure. He says:

> दण्डयस्यादण्डनान्नित्यमदण्डस्य च दण्डनात्।
> अतिदण्डाच्च गुणिभिस्त्यज्यते पातकी भवेत।।
> (Dandyasādandnānnityamdandasya ca dandnāt
> Atidandācca gunibhištyjyate pātaki bhavet)
>
> — *Śukra Nitih (4-1-52)*
>
> *Not punishing the one who should be punished every day and punishing a person who should not be punished and punishing excessively are all unreasonable acts. The learned ones renounce the King doing so.*

The above policy suggests that the *dand* strategy must be a well-considered one. If the culprits remain unpunished and innocent ones get punished, the basic principle of law gets flouted. Existence of such state of affairs and continuance thereof is bound to lead the whole system to destruction. So the case of excessive punishment is fatal not only for the King but also for anyone who practises that.

This one couplet would provide a lot of wisdom to the managers and administrators, who often have to make use of the *dand* strategy. The strategy is not free from serious complications. Any unwise use may create serious problems, which may take long to resolve.

Conclusion

These four *upāyās* discussed by Śukra are widely referred to in various scriptures. These strategies are mostly used but their scientific basis is hardly known. In day-to-day life situations, work situations and otherwise, these are extensively practised. However, practising a policy with its scientific knowledge or rationale behind it is always better, because the person using them knows its pitfalls and advantages.

The knowledge about the four *upāyās* is ancient, yet they are being used successfully even in the modern times. They have really stood the test of time and have remained untarnished by the advanced technology. The *upāyās* lead on the way from success to success as milestones of winning over the people.

OO

8

Crisis Management
(Hanuman —The Great Crisis Manager)

Emergence of the Thought

Rapid development of technology has developed the art and science of management into various finer branches. Crisis Management is one of them. Almost all living beings and so also organisations face awkward, dangerous or serious situations, decisive moments, turning points and these are precisely the moments of crisis. If handled with wisdom, clarity and objectivity, crisis may be gainfully used or else may lead to ruins. The deft ones survive, others succumb.

A Way of Life

Crisis needs to be treated only as a way of life, which if not sprinkled with struggles may not be worth living. Indian way of life is:

> कुर्वन्नेवेह कर्माणि जिजीविषेत् शतं समाः ।
> (Kurvanneveh karmāni ĵijīviset śtaḿ samāḥ)
>
> — *Vạjsyèn Yajurved (40-2), Iśopnishad (2)*
>
> *One may live for one hundred years and may indulge in good deeds in the spirit of yajňya.*

This is a Vedic injunction. The one, who lives Vedas, indulges in *Karma* (action) as *yajňya.* It is through *yajňya* that one respects the superiors, binds and serves the society, helps the needy and uplifts the downtrodden. For such a person, birth is essential. It is a means to action or *Karma* and a dispenser of joy and happiness. If there is no birth, no life, then where is the action? Then, of course, there is no crisis. So crisis is a natural phenomenon and the test of intellect and courage. Therefore, it is a positive force and ought to be taken as such. Besides that there is hardly a way out as crisis must come in most lives. The Vedic way of life takes them as natural consequence, and so should all of us. Hanuman's lifestyle was Vedic. He always led his life in the spirit of *yajňya* and dealt with crises without losing his clam.

Crisis I

In *Ramayana*, Hanuman appears on the scene as a minister of Sugrīva, the younger brother of Bali, the King of Kiśkindha. He was a favourite of Sugrīva to the extent that he always lived with him when he (Sugrīva) was passing his days as a fugitive for fear of Bali.

Sugrīva, in the hills of Riṣýamūkh, saw Sri Ram and Lakśman from a great distance and was scared that they might be Bali's agents. This was the crisis for the thought that if they were so he may run away and seek refuge elsewhere. In the moments of such crisis, he sought Hanuman's support.

Hanuman had a difficult task to perform. It involved dealing with strangers to assess who they were and what was their mission, if possible to win them over to Sugrīva's side. Any mistake or misjudgement could change the picture. Hanuman could make up his mind how to accomplish the goal. He dealt with the two brothers so wisely and skilfully that both the parties could perceive the success of their mission in one another. It was mainly on account of such skill that Hanuman came to be adorned with the adjectives, like '*Vākya Kushal*', '*Vākya Viśārd*' and possessing '*Slaksanám Madhuryā Girā*'. Sri Ram had all praises for the dexterity that Hanuman possessed. The skill with which Hanuman used the *sam* and *dan* efforts, made Lakśman to say that the joy and cheerfulness with which Hanuman talks makes one to perceive that he never tells lies. Hanuman had complete control over his speech. He had clear ideas where to speak and where to keep quiet to let the other party speak. So, after he finished his narration, Valmiki says:

एवमुकत्वा तु हनुमांस्तौ वीरौ राम लक्ष्मणौ ।
वाक्यज्ञौ वाक्यकुशलः पुनर्नोवाच किंचित । ।

(Evamuktvā tu Hanumānstau virau Rām Lakśhmanau
Vākyajňau vākyakushlah punarnovāch kincit)

— Ramayana Kiśkindha Kand (3-24)

Saying so to Sri Ram and Lakśman, wise in speaking,brave and 'vakya kushal' Hanuman kept quiet and said nothing thereafter.

Now it was for Sri Ram and Lakśman to speak and so they did. Wisdom, at that juncture, demanded the other person to speak.

Thus convinced with the request of Hanuman, to be friendly with Sugrīva and to protect him, he brought Sri Ram and Lakśman to Sugrīva's abode on the hills, yet he did not bring them face to face unless he had talked to Sugrīva, who when convinced, came to receive Sri Ram.

The friendship was announced informally but Hanuman preferred to give a religion binding to it; so he lit the holy fire, which both parties worshipped. Thereafter:

तयोर्मध्येऽथ सुप्रीते निदधे सुसमाहितः ।
ततोऽग्निं दीप्यमानं तौ चक्रतुश्च प्रदक्षिणम ।।

(Tyormdhyeth suprite nidadhe susamahitah
Tatoagnim dipyamanam tau cakratusca pradaksinam)

— *Ramayana Kiśkindha Kand (5-16)*

Crisis I Resolved

After the fire was lit between Sri Ram and Sugrīva and the fire started giving flames, both went round it. This ritual of going round the fire in flames has always been treated as a binding force. The fire (an element of nature) becomes a witness. In Hindu Marriage system, going round the fire in flames is a must. This acts as a moral and spiritual force to the relationship. So Hanuman did not miss even such details.

Crisis II

Thus, when Sri Ram completed his obligations towards Sugrīva, who was installed as the King of Kiśkindha after Sri Ram killed Bali, the rainy season had set in. It was settled that after the rains, Sugrīva would make all his efforts to locate Sita. But indulging in sensuous pleasures, Sugrīva forgot his words. Then again, there was a crisis. Hanuman had forewarned Sugrīva on this account, yet he did not pay heed to that. Thus infuriated Lakśman, on the instructions of Sri Ram, came to Kiśkindha; again there was a crisis to be taken care by Hanuman.

Crisis II Resolved

Hanuman inspired Sugrīva, who sent his search parties in all directions. The south was to be taken care of by the party in which Hanuman was there, led by Angada, the son of Bali and the crown prince. When this party was about to leave for south, Sri Ram had no difficulty in visualising Hanuman to be successful in the mission. So he gave his ring as an insignia to him and also the message for Sita, and the party left to come back after a month or so.

Two Minor Crises

While on reconnaissance, the party came across a situation when all the party members were tired, thirsty and hungry. They saw a dark deep cave in the mountain. It was shrouded with mystery and none had the courage to enter it. It was Hanuman who saw birds flying in and out of it and so imagined that some source of water must be inside. He led the party in the cave where they all got water and fruits in plenty and lived there comfortably for a few days. Then the sage Svyam Prabha sent them to the seashore with the help of her mystical powers.

On the seashore, the party was against yet another crisis. A giant vulture, Sampāti, who was very hungry, saw the party members as his food. Here again it was Hanuman's presence of mind that resolved the crisis. He loudly started talking about another giant vulture, Jatāyu who laid his life to accomplish Sri Ram's mission. This Jatāyu happened to be the brother of Sampāti. When Sampāti, on asking, was told about Jatāyu's story, he promised help to the exploring party. It was then Sampāti, who being a vulture, had a very distant sight, saw Sita in Lanka. It was thus that a minor crisis was over and the added gain was the gain of a clue about Sita to the party. But now there was a bigger crisis.

Resolving the Big Crisis

Having the knowledge about Sita being in Lanka, the problem was to find a warrior who could cross the hundred *yojan* sea, find the whereabouts of Sita in Lanka and then come back. All the warriors boasted about their powers to cross the sea but none was confident about the hundred *yojan* leap to cross. Then Angada, the team leader, said that he was ready to cross. But old Jambvant was not in favour of sending the crown prince, as he had Hanuman in his view. So he approached him and said:

वीर वानरलोकस्य सर्वशास्त्र विशारद।
तूष्णीमेकान्तमाश्रित्य हनुमन किं न जल्पसि।।
(Vir vānarloksya sarvaśāstra viśārad
Tūṣṇīmekāntmaśritya Hanuman kim na jalpasi)

— Ramayana Kiśkindha Kand (66-2)

O! Brave one, well-versed in all branches of knowledge, Hanuman, why are you sitting alone, why do you not say something?

Then Jambvant talked about the high deeds of his father and his own abilities, upon which Hanuman showed his readiness to accomplish the task. He then disclosed his abilities and mentally reached Lanka; ultimately he took the great leap from the top of a hill.

On his way to Lanka, over the sea, Hanuman succeeded in three tests that one has to take while performing an uphill task. Surasa came to test his intelligence and readiness, Mainak came to test his stamina and Singhika to test his strength. Hanuman emerged victorious in all the three.

On crossing the sea, Hanuman climbed the Lamb Mountain to wait for a while. This too was wise act as he could survey Lanka only from a height. Moreover, Lanka was built on Trikut Hills. Valmiki has vividly described Lanka as seen by Hanuman from the Lamb Mountain. Then he decided to wait till the sunset. After it was dark, Hanuman assumed a miniature body, like that of a cat. In this context, it has been said:

सूर्य चांस्ते गते रात्रौ देहं सांक्षिप्य मारुतिः ।
वृषदंशकमात्रः सम्बभूवाम्द तदर्शनः ।।
(Surya cānste gate rātro deham sakṣipya maruth̤
vriṣdanśkmatraḥ sambbhubadbha tadarśnaḥ)

— Ramayana Sundar Kand (3-48)

After sunset when it was dark, he adopted the miniature form of the size of a mystic cat.

In such a miniature form, when Hanuman was entering Lanka, he was challenged by Lankini (the Goddess of Lanka). There was some dialogue and ultimately Lankini was badly hit and vomited blood. Then, realising the situation, Lankini permitted him to go into Lanka wherever he wished.

After he entered Lanka, Hanuman made a detailed survey of the town and the houses therein. He went from house to house in the mission to get an idea about the town, the lifestyle there, and the whereabouts of Sita. It was early morning by the time he finished his survey and collected information to locate Sita. He went to the Ashoka Vatika where he had a glimpse of Sita. He quietly climbed a tree to wait for the appropriate opportunity.

Meanwhile, Ravana came and tried to force Sita to become his queeen. But when Sita refused and rebuked him, he posted some fearsome women to scare her to the extent that she may accept the proposal, but all in vain. The fearful ones then went here and there, and thus Hanuman got the proper occasion. At this stage, instead of appearing before Sita, he created suspense. He recited words of appreciation for Sri Ram, Lakśman and Daśratha. Listening to that, Sita wanted to know, who was saying all that. After that much of suspense, Hanuman appeared and narrated all the details. Then he gave the ring to Sita, which Sri Ram had given as insignia. At last, Sita was convinced that he was Sri Ram's emissary. She was much relieved of the tension. Hanuman then gave Sri Ram's message to Sita and assured her that Sri Ram would come to Lanka soon and get her free from Ravana's captivity. He demanded some insignia from her so that Sri Ram may be convinced that the real Sita has been located. Sita gave her *cūdámani* (hair ornament studded with precious stones) as an insignia and thereafter Hanuman took leave of her.

Greater Diffusion

Though, in a way, the major part of Hanuman's mission of locating Sita was accomplished, yet a part was still to be completed. He wanted to demoralise the Lankans, which in his view would help much, when Sri Ram would attack Lanka. He thought of the four *upāyās*, *sam*, *dan*, *bhed*, and *dand*, and concluded that *sam* and *dan* may not be effective. He ultimately decided on *dand*, which in turn was *bhed* in operation. Deciding so, he ruined the Ashoka Vatika, which was so dear to Ravana. The guards and protectors were killed. Those who escaped sent the information to Ravana, who thereafter sent his forces, but they were also killed. Then Ravana's son Prahasta was sent and he too was killed in the encounter with Hanuman. Finally came Meghnad who fought for a long time without success. At last, he hit Hanuman with *Brahmastra* (weapon given by Brahma). Showing respect to *Brahma*, Hanuman accepted its injury and was caught, tied with chains and presented before Ravana.

Hanuman talked to Ravana fearlessly and revealed his own self and the mission. Ravana ordered his killing, but his brother Vibhiśana advised that emissaries must not be killed, according to the accepted principles of statecraft. So the punishment of burning Hanuman's tail was ordered and executed. Hanuman used the fire in his tail to burn the houses of the Lankans and scare them. After turning the town into ashes, Hanuman put off the fire in the sea. He then announced his identity and mission, went back to Sri Ram and narrated all the happenings. This is how he resolved the crises one by one. Brilliance of Hanuman as a crisis manager can be visualised by the fact that he always resolved the crisis, big or small, and went much ahead of that. For example, he not only located Sita but also collected information about Lanka, judged the strength of Ravana and demoralised the Lankans, which was helpful in the final battle when Lanka was attacked.

Extra Efforts

Such wisdom of Hanuman in performing the principal task of emissary and then doing something extra is a great ability. Describing theses qualities, Valmiki has said:

> कार्ये कर्मणि निर्दिष्टे यो बहून्यपि साधयेत।
> पूर्वकार्या विरोधेन स कार्यं कर्तुमर्हति।।
> (Kārye karmani nirdiṣte yo bahunapi sādhyet
> pūrva kāryā virodhena sa kāryaṁ kartumarhāti)
>
> — *Ramayana Sundar Kand (42-5)*

> *First accomplishing the main task and without adversely affecting that of the emissary, he performs other tasks that are allied ones, so that the emissary is really worthy of being called an able emissary.*

This was exactly the method adopted by Hanuman as discussed earlier. Then Valmiki takes another virtue akin to the one just described. He says:

> यो ह्येकः साधको हेतुः स्वल्पस्यापीह कर्मणः।
> यो ह्यर्थं बहुधा वेद स समर्थोऽर्थसाधने।।
> (Yo hyekaḥ sādhako hētuḥ svalpāsyapih karmanaḥ
> yo hyarthaiṁ bahudhā ved sa samrthoarthsādhane)
>
> — *Ramayana Sundar Kand (42-6)*

The one, who completes some paltry assignment by great efforts, is not the real doer of things. But the one who accomplishes his assignment and the connected works too, with ordinary efforts is the real and effective doer.

In this view, Hanuman thought that if he leaves Lanka without making a mark, that would not be helpful. The Lankans, their warriors and finally Ravana would never realise the possible strength of Sri Ram and his army, if he goes back without giving them a taste of it. He, therefore, decided to use the *dand* method and caused such destruction and killings, which left an indelible mark not only on the Lankans, their warriors and Ravana, but also scared the women and children greatly. All of that came under the *bhed upāyā* (method). Amongst themselves, they started feeling and saying that Ravana made a great mistake in abducting Sita for his own pleasure, ignoring the larger interests. This was the brightness of Hanuman's strategy. He was not only a crisis resolving person, but a brilliant emissary and an excellent planner, executor and general. Any mistake by Hanuman in handling the crisis situation or accomplishing the allied jobs could have frustrated the whole purpose and changed the shape of the happenings altogether. That is the reason Valmiki chose to adorn him with the adjective, *'Sarve śastravid'* *(सर्व शास्त्रविदं)*.

Foresight

The happenings show that Ravana might have ordered Hanuman to be killed; he opened a channel to check that. When Ravana asked him, who he was, Hanuman said:

निवेदयामास हरीश्वरस्य ।
दूतः सकाशादध्मागतोऽस्मि ।।
(Nivedyāmās hariśvarasya
dūtaḥ sakāśādadhmāgatosmi)

— *Ramayana Sundar Kand (51-61)*

In reply, Hanuman said that he was the ambassador of King Sugrīva and had come from him.

Hanuman's wisdom demanded that he must identify himself as an ambassador of a king, only then, he could escape death sentence, and so he did. Taking advantage of such introduction, Vibhiśana could plead that the diplomatic principles demand that an ambassador should not be killed. Such pleading played a dual purpose. Hanuman was saved and he got a chance to destroy Lanka. Thus, in the process of resolving the crisis situations Hanuman exhibited foresight, which was helpful in defusing the danger, which at one stage appeared to be inevitable.

Medicine to Defuse Crisis

During the battle in Lanka, there came a day when Meghnad fought so valiantly that Sri Ram and Lakśman, struck by *Brahmastra*, lay unconscious in the battlefield. Most of the warriors of Sri Ram force lay injured in a semi-conscious state and a high number of soldiers were killed. Pandemonium prevailed in the battlefield. Meghnad was almost victorious. Hanuman and Vibhiśana decided to go to the injured warriors, one by one, to cheer them up and to boost up their morale; while they were in the process of doing so, they met the great general Jambvant, who on seeing Vibhiśana, enquired the well-being of Hanuman. On such asking, Vibhiśana questioned that instead of enquiring about the health of Sri Ram or Lakśman, why he showed his concern about Hanuman. Replying to Vibhiśana's question, Jambvant said:

> तस्मिन् जीवति वीरे तु हतमप्यहतं बलम् ।
> हनुमत्युज्झितप्राणे जीवन्तोऽपि वयं हताः ।।
> धरते मारुतिस्तात मारुतप्रतिमो यदिः ।
> वैश्वानरसमो वीर्ये जीविताशा ततो भवेत् ।।
> (Tasmin jivati vīre tu hatmapyajataṁ balam,
> Hanmatyujijhatprāne jianto pi vayam hatāḥ
> Darte mārutistāt mārut pratimo yadiḥ
> Vaiśvānarsamo virye jivitāśā tato bhavet)
>
> — *Ramayana Yuddha Kand (74-22, 74-23)*

If Hanuman is alive then despite being killed, the whole army is alive and if ever Hanuman dies then take it that even the alive ones are as good as dead. If, swift as wind and mighty as fire Hanuman is alive, then I am hopeful of the life of even the dead ones.

Then, Hanuman went to Jambvant, the old general, and touching his feet saluted him. On this, though in great agony due to injuries, the King of Bears, Jambvant, recognising the voice of Hanuman visualised his rebirth. He asked Hanuman to save the lives of the soldiers and warriors, Sri Ram and Lakśman. He advised that much above the sea level is the mountain Himalayas and on that is a hill by the name 'Ṛṣbha'(ऋषभ)

from where you can see the Kailash mount. In between the two you will find shining herbs which illumine the whole area these are 'Mritsanjīvani' (मृतसंजीविनी), 'Vishalya karni' (विशाल्यकरणीह्व), 'Savarn karni' (सावर्णकरणी) and 'Sandhan karni' (संधानकरणी) which respectively make the dead one alive, heal the wounds, remove the ugly tone of wounds and bind the skin over the wounds. Jambvant asked Hanuman to bring those medicines and give life to all.

As advised, Hanuman left for Himalayas at once. On the pointed hill, not finding the herbs, he lifted the hill itself and brought it to the battlefield, where the herbs were plucked. On smelling the herbs, Sri Ram and Lakśman regained consciousness, the wounds and injuries of the warriors healed up and all were fit once again. Thereafter Hanuman lifted the hill once again and placed it at its original situation and spot. Thus, Hanuman was once again successful in defusing yet another crisis.

Medicine Needed Again

However, the crises keep arising one after the other. In the final stage of the battle, Lakśman sustained serious injuries and was in an unconscious state. On Vibhiśana's advice, Sri Ram called Vaidya Suşen from Lanka and requested him to cure Lakśman. Who else was there to help and accelerate the process? Hanuman was the only known one to defuse the crisis. So Vaidya Suşen requested him:

सौम्य शीघ्रमितो गत्वा शैलमोषिधपर्वतम् ।
पूर्वं ते कथितो योऽसौ वीर जाम्बवता शुभः ।।
दक्षिणे शिखरे तस्य जात मोषाधिमानय ।।

(Saumya śigramito gatvā śailmoşidh parvatam
Parvaṁ te kthito yosyau vir Jambvatā śubhah
Dakşne śikhare tasya jatmoşdhi mānaya)

— *Ramayana Yuddha Kand (122-21)*

O! Dear one, go at once to the mountain earlier identified by Jambvant and from the south hilltop, bring the herbs medicines.

Then Hanuman at once acted as per the advice of Vaidya Suşen. He again brought the entire hill. The herbs were taken out, medicine prepared and administered. Lakśman regained consciousness and was cured. The hill was again replaced at its original place. On this rebirth of

Lakśman, everyone was extremely joyous and happy. Such act of Hanuman has been appreciated thus:

दृष्टवा हनुमतः कर्म सुरैरपि सुदुष्करम् ।

(Driṣtvā Hanumataḥ karma suraiŕapi saduṣkaram)

— *Ramayana Yuddha Kand (102-35)*

Seeing Hanuman perform the job, which was difficult for even the Devatas, the soldiers became happy and joyful.

Crisis Diffuser

The exemplary capacity of Hanuman in facing the crises and defusing them were extraordinary. Such quality of Hanuman was appreciated by everyone. The famous poet Tulsidas in the 16th century A.D. composed a poem of eight stanzas in which he adorned Hanuman as *sankat mochan*, the reliever from the crisis. And this is no exaggeration, as Hanuman being a front line crisis manager was a person of vision, foresight and intelligence. He won acclaim not only from his own people but also from the enemies. Such respect in the opposite camp was based on past deeds of Hanuman.

The use of *dand* in Lanka after meeting Sita in Ashoka Vatika had created a lasting impact on Lankans. This is an established instance followed by two other examples.

Firstly when Sri Ram's army was camping outside Lanka, Sri Ram sent Angada, Bali's son, as an emissary of peace to Ravana. Angada entered Lanka and to his utter dismay noticed that on his very sight most Lankans appeared to be scared as they ran inside their houses. The women and children would not come out. This was only the effect of the destruction of Lanka, which Hanuman had done, in his very first visit.

Secondly, when after the final victory over Ravana, Sri Ram sent Hanuman to bring Sita, the reception bestowed upon him by the Lankans was:

इति प्रतिसमादिष्टो हनुमान मारुतात्मजः ।
प्रतिवेश पुरीं लंकां पूज्यमानो निशाचरैः ।।

(Iti pratisamādiṣtau Hanumān mārutātmajaḥ
Prativeś purim Lankām pūjymāno niśacariḥ)

When as per directions of Sri Ram, Hanuman went into Lanka then the people of Lanka gave him a rousing welcome and paid their high regards.

The word '*pūjyamāno*' draws attention. It means that they treated Hanuman so respectfully as to be worshipped. This was the result of the deeds of Hanuman that he performed not just for diffusing the crisis but also as additional work. The crisis at that time was to locate and find out about Sita, which was over when Hanuman found Sita and conversed with her. He could have come back to Sri Ram, but his wisdom demanded to do something else also so as to leave an impression on Lankans about him.

Behavioural Scientist Valmiki

The penultimate crisis was to assess Bharat's attitude towards Sri Ram and the Kingdom of Ayodhya. Bharat had been at the helm of affairs for fourteen long years. The possibilities of a change in his attitude could not be brushed aside. So Sri Ram wanted to ascertain the situation before reaching Ayodhya. He, therefore, summoned Hanuman, the wisest one and said:

तत्त्वेन मुखवर्णेन् दृष्टया व्याभरणेण च।

(Tattven mukhvarnena dṛstya vyabharnen ca)

— *Ramayana Yuddha Kand (128-14)*

You narrate the news of my coming back and then observe the expressions on the face and eyes of Bharat and also what he says.

Some people may consider this act as not matching Sri Ram's temperament. Yet it is very akin to the basic tenets of behavioural science. It was the insight of Valmiki in the principles of behavioural science that prompted him to get such words from Sri Ram. Valmiki was so sagacious that he made Sri Ram to direct only Hanuman to make observations on Bharat's face and eyes. It was left to Hanuman to draw conclusion. This shows the wisdom of Hanuman in the area of behavioural science. Sri Ram had directed Hanuman to come back to him only if he noticed some change. Thus the incident exhibits the prudence and keen knowledge of Valmiki regarding the complicated principles of behavioural science. Such an enquiry was necessary in the social interest.

Sri Ram was aware of the capabilities of all his generals. It was on that basis that he chose Hanuman for this assignment, which required high degree of intelligence and wisdom.

Hanuman, at once left for this new assignment. He went to Bharat, gave him news of Sri Ram's arrival. He closely watched the expression on the face and eyes and what he said. Watching all the reactions, Hanuman was completely satisfied that there was no change at all in Bharat's affection and reverence towards Sri Ram, Sita and Lakśman. He, therefore, had no reason to go back to Sri Ram and make a report. Thus, once again a crisis was resolved successfully. This was done by Hanuman as per directions of Sri Ram.

Though, Valmiki's deep insight into the principles of behavioural science is visible at many places, but here he has shown his excellence which fits well in to the modern trends.

A question arises as to why Sri Ram sent Hanuman to assess the attitude of Bharat and what social good was involved in such act. This aspect can be appreciated from the fact that firstly Sri Ram had so much of affection for Bharat that at no cost he wanted Bharat to see displeased. The other reason was that if the people of Ayodhya were happy in Bharat's rule and did not feel the absence of Sri Ram, there was no point in disturbing the social system. It was the Vedic order that in performance of all duties (*Dharma*), the social interest must be considered as supreme. All such points in view, Valmiki dealt with this topic which not only highlights the characters of Sri Ram and Bharat, but also exhibits the expertise of Hanuman in the principles of behavioural science, and ultimately of Valmiki which matches with the modern trend.

Sublimed Ego

Hanuman had a notable quality of being an altruist to the core. This quality can be observed anywhere and everywhere. He had no mission of his own. All that he did was for social good, which can be summed up as 'victory of goodness over evil'.

After victory over Ravana, Sri Ram chose Hanuman to go to Lanka to bring Sita. Hanuman, then, pleasantly appeared before Sita and gave her the news of Sri Ram's victory. He said that the Sri Ram had called her. On hearing this news, Sita was overjoyed and said that she could not conceive anything on the earth, which she could treat as a suitable reward for such a great news. She wanted to give away all precious things. On this, Hanuman said:

स्निग्धमेतंविधं वाक्यं त्वमेवार्हसि भाषितुम् ।
तथैतद्वचनं सौम्ये सारवत् स्निग्धमेव च ।
रत्नौघाद्विधाच्चापि देवराज्याद्विशिष्यते ।
अर्थतश्च मया प्राप्ता देवराज्यादयो गुणाः ।।

(Snigdhametam vidham vākyam tvamevarhasi bhāśitum
Tathaitava vacanam saumye sārvat snigdhamev ca
Ranaughā dvidāccāpi devarājyādviśşyate
Arthtaśca mayā prāptā devrājyādayo gunāḥ)

— *Ramayana Yuddha Kand (116-23, 24)*

O! Pious one, it is only your gracious self who can say such affectionate, captivating and meaningful words. These words are more valuable than a variety of precious stones and also the Kingdom of Heavens. This humble one has received greater joy as compared to all the precious things of the world. I find Sri Ram happy again and that is my greatest reward.

In this chapter, Valmiki's *Ramayana* has been taken as the basis. No comparisons have been made between the principles contemplated by modern thinkers on management of crises. It has been done so mainly for two reasons. Firstly, crisis management as a branch of management science is of recent origin. The principles may vary from crisis to crisis. The second reason is that Hanuman so successfully resolved and defused such varied crises that their study and thinking provokes a thoughtful mind on its own. In this chapter, different crises have been described briefly along with the process of their resolution that a thinking mind can apply them with suitable amends.

It can be said on visualising and judging the deeds of Hanuman that he was a great crisis manager possessing immense wisdom and intelligence. Tulsidas has rightly named him as '*sankat mochan*' (संकटमोचन).

The crises described in this chapter are practical cases along with their solutions. They may prove useful and helpful to the modern managers possessing insight into the behavioural science. The crises discussed herein are of varying nature and shades, so also the different ways of their resolution.

○○

9

Manage Your Speaking (The Science and Art of Speaking)

Speaking

Speaking is 'sharing of goal-oriented messages between persons, to meet the target'. It is one of the means of transmitting messages. Spoken words can evoke pride, loyalty, action or silence. They can exalt, praise, pray, insult, injure, create false hopes and illusion, and even lead to costly and serious errors.

The art of speaking is a science, in which nothing succeeds which is not planned. Therefore, speaking needs great care by the captains in industry, the managers, who spend more time in communicating as compared to the other activities.

What matters is not what is said but how it is said, heard and understood. People react not to what is said but what the listener thinks has been said. The factors that have a bearing on speaking and its correct understanding are very many, such as, the time, occasion, situation, pitch, modulation, facial expression, body language, movement of eyes, usage of words, the style, the audience, speaker's personality, the object, and purpose, when to stop and when not to speak at all, etc. etc.

The art of speaking may be understood, as control of speech, appropriate speaking and discipline of speaking, '*Vani/Vak Sanyam*'. All these aspects have been adequately appreciated and deliberated upon by Indian thinkers of the remote past, in the scriptures like *Mahabharata*, *Śukra Nitih*, *Manu Smriti*, Kautilya's *Artha Śastra* and many others.

Controlled Speaking

In *Mahabharata*, referring to the '*vak sanyam*', Vidur says:

वाकसंयमो हि नृपते सुदुष्करतमो गतः ।
अर्थवद विचित्रं च न शक्यं बहु भाषितम् ।।
(Vāksamymo hi nṛpate sudaşkarṭamo gataḥ
Arthavad Vicitraṁ ca na śukyaṁ bahu bhāşitam)

— *Mahabharata Udyog Parva (34-76)*

Complete control over speaking is very difficult; but meaningful speech too is not possible for long. Control over speech is achieved by long practice and that too for some length of time.

Control over speaking '*vak sanyam*' here means meaningful and wonderful speech to be continued for long.

More important aspect of control of speech is that the speaker ought to know where to stop speaking and where not to speak at all. One cannot speak well, who does not know how to hold his pace.

Timely Speaking

The skill of speaking calls for many considerations. One of them is to understand and appreciate the proper time and occasion. Highlighting this, Vidura says:

अप्राप्त कालं वचनं बृहस्पतिरपि ब्रूवन ।
लभते बुद्धय वज्ञानम् वमानम् च भारत ।।
(Aprāpta kālaṁ vacanaṁ bṛhaspatirapi bruvan,
Labhatc buddhaya vajñānam vamānam ca bhārat)

— *Mahabharata Udyog Parva (39)*

If, even Bṛhaspati (the guru of Devtas), speaks at an inappropriate time, he will be insulted and his intellect shall not be cared for.

Untimely Speaking

The couplet gives the example of an intellectual of the highest order. Even a great intellectual speaking at an inappropriate time and juncture can be on the onslaught of humiliation, what to say of the ordinary and average person. It is mainly on this account that wise persons remain quiet till the proper occasion, when the audience is prone to listen. A famous saying goes, 'A closed mouth gathers no fool'.

Examples are many to show that speaking even the truth at an improper occasion, situation and time may place the speaker in serious troubles. The famous Sanskrit teaching is:

सत्यं ब्रूयात प्रियं ब्रूयात न ब्रूयात सत्यमप्रियम्।

(Satyam brūyāt priyam brūyāt na brūyāt satyamapriyam)

Speak the truth, speak pleasant things, and do not speak the unpleasant truth.

The injunction does not provide for speaking lie, in case of an unpleasant truth. The real intent is to keep quiet, if the truth is unpleasant. The wisdom lies in deciding to remain quiet on inopportune moments.

The Language

Deliberating upon the pleasant and unpleasant language, Vidura says:

अभ्याभवति कल्याणं विविध वाक् सुभाषिता।

सैव दुर्भाषिता राजन्नानार्था योप पद्यते।।

(Abhābhavati kalyānaṁ vivid vāk subhāşitā
Saiva durbhāşitā rājannanārthā yop padyte)

— *Mahabharata Udyog Parva (34-77)*

Something said in sweet and pleasant language is beneficial in many ways. But, if said in harsh words, it may be the cause for many troubles.

Calling a blind man as '*soordas ji*' does not sound harsh. However, calling the same person '*andha*' causes offence. Similar views have been expressed by Manu.

Injury is Caused

In *Mahabharata*, it has been said:

रोहते सायकैर्विद्धं वनम् परषुना हतम्।

वाचा दुरुक्तं बीभत्सम् न संरोहति वाकक्षतम्।।

(Rohate sāykairviddhaṁ vanam parşunā hatam
Vācā duruktam bībhatsam na sanrohāti vākkştam)

— *Mahabharata Udyog Parva (34-78)*

Pierced by arrows and cut by axe, the jungle becomes green once again; but the injury caused by harsh words is so serious that it does not heal up.

In this couplet, the word 'injury' has been used. The injury caused by words has been termed as 'verbal injury', which is many times more painful than the physical injury. Sometimes, the spoken words cause such deep injury that the listener is not able to tolerate. Possibly, he may retaliate with vengeance and may resort to extreme steps.

Killing Phrases

In man-management area, the usage of 'killing phrases' by the manager also gets classified as verbal injury. A manager, telling the subordinate, 'you are a useless person', 'this job is beyond your capacity', and 'better talk sense', etc. tend to create such negative effect that the listener may become a non-performer. It has, therefore, been noticed that able and competent managers refrain from using humiliating and harsh words with their subordinates. On the contrary, they maintain the dignity of their subordinates at a high level.

Injuring Language

Elaborating further about not using injuring language, Śukra has said:

हृधि विद्ध इवात्यर्थं यथा संतप्यते जनः ।
पण्डितोऽपि हि मेधावी न तां वाचमुदीरयेत। ।

(Hridhi viddha ivātyrtham yathā santapyate janah,

Pandidoapi he medhāvi na tam vācamudiryat)

— *Śukra Nitih (1-167)*

While in difficulties and calamities, the wise man should not speak in such words and language, which may injure and cause pain to the listener.

Such is the discipline of speaking that even in adverse situation one ought to use well-composed language. The real test of a wise and disciplined person is to maintain poise in abnormal circumstances, because, it has been noticed that many balanced persons lose their mental equilibrium in trying situations. However, those who have sufficiently practised self-discipline stand like mountains in the adversities.

Verbal Injury

Verbal injury gets caused by spoken words and language. Such injury is so painful that even matured persons get deeply hurt and are prone to commit ugly and heinous acts. Defining verbal injury, Kautilya has said:

वाक्पारुष्यम् उपवाद कुत्सनमभिभर्त्सनमिति ।
(Vākpāruṣyam upvād kutsnambhibhartonamiti)

— Artha Śastra (3-18-1)

Defamation, vilification and threat constitute verbal injuries.

After naming the three types of verbal injuries, Kautilya in his style of a teacher, explains each type. Thus explaining, he has said the defamation may pertain to body, character, learning, profession and country. An example of defamation in relation to body may be like calling someone '*kana*' (one-eyed), '*langra*' (lame), '*andha*' (blind) etc.

Vilification may be in relation to leprosy, madness, impotence, false or ironical praise, such as 'How beautiful eyes!' for a squint, etc.

Regarding threat, the example is:

एवं त्वाम् करिष्यामि ।
(Evam tvām kariṣyami)

— Artha Śastra (3-18-1)

'I shall see you.'

Kautilya not only enumerates the verbal injuries but also prescribes punishments in the shape of fines. In case of defamation pertaining to body, such as calling someone '*kana*' the fine was three *panas*, if the defect was a fact in case the imputation was false, the fine was six *panas*.

Manu's Views

Deliberating upon verbal injuries, Manu has said:

काणं वाप्यथवा खंजनमन्यं वापि तथा विधम् ।
तथ्येनापि ब्रुवन्दाप्यो दण्ड कार्षापणा वरम् । ।
(Kanaṁ vāpyathvā khanjanmanyaṁ vāpi tathā vidham
Tathyenāpi bruvundāpyo danda kārṣāpanā varam)

— Manu Smriti (8-274)

Anybody calling 'kana' to a one-eyed person or with any deficiency is liable to a fine up to one karshapana.

Dealing with other forms of verbal injuries, Manu says:

हीनांगा नति रिक्तांगान्विद्याहीनान्वयोधिकान् ।
रूप दिव्यं विहीनांश्च जातिहीनांश्च नाक्षिपेत । ।

(Hīnāngā nati riktanganvidya hinanvayo dhikan
Rup divyam vihinanśca jatihinanşca nakşipet)

— *Manu Smriti (4-141)*

One should never cut injuring jokes, cause defamation or vilification to the persons who may be short of limbs or have extra ones, the uneducated elders, the ugly, poor or lower caste persons; causing verbal injury to such persons by joking or humiliating has been treated as offence punishable with fine.

In Manu's view, calling names to low caste was punishable. However some of the modern leaders paint a distorted image of Manu as a top enemy of low castes, which is far from the fact, in view of the data.

Sukra's Views

Extending the thought further, Śukra goes to the extent that harsh words should not be used even for the closest ones, like wife and children.

कदापि नोग्र दण्डः स्यात कटुभाषणं तत्परः ।
भार्या पुत्रोऽप्युद्विजते कटुवाक्यादुग्र दण्डतः ।।

(Kadāpi nogra dandaḥ syat katubhaşnḿ tatparaḥ
Bharya putroapyudvijate katu vakyadugra dandataḥ)

— *Śukra Nitih (3-85)*

Harsh and injurious words should not be spoken or severe punishment may not be given even to the members of the family. Even the closer ones, like wife and children, cannot tolerate insulting and humiliating language, how can others, like neighbours, friends and subordinates be expected to listen and tolerate such language?

Tabooed Speaking

Harsh, humiliating and insulting language coming from even high and rich persons is not relished, as the same causes anguish to the listener. Therefore, use of hurting language has been considered tabooed for all.

नित्यं मनोपहारिण्या वाचा प्रहलादयेज्जगत ।
उद्वेजयति भूतानि क्रूरवाग्घनेदोऽपि सन ।।

(Nityaḿ manophārinyā vācā prahlādyejjagat
Udvejayati bhūtāni krurvāgdhnadōpi san)

— *Śukra Nitih (1-166)*

One should please everyone with sweet words, the person giving wealth may be the richest one, but by harsh words, he causes pain and injury and thus does great harm to others.

The principle can be applied to normal self-respecting people, not to abnormal and greedy ones. A person with self-respect intact may not accept money in return of insult and humiliation. Therefore, prudent people refrain from speaking undesirable words.

Prescribing, what one should desist from speaking, it has been said:

कस्यचिन्त स्पृशेन्मर्म मिथ्या वादं न कस्यचित ।

Kasyacinna spṛśnmarma mithyā vādam na kasyacit)

— *Śukra Nitih (3-64)*

Do not speak to any person, the words which may cause pain. Refrain from telling lies to any one.

Use of the 'marma sparśi' (मर्म स्पर्शी) words denotes such words that touch the heart in a negative manner. Usually the satirical expressions do hurt the heart. Such words and expressions cause pain. Therefore, they should not be spoken.

Then, there are obscene and abusive expressions, which are tabooed:

नाश्लीलं कीर्तयेत कंचित प्रलापं न च कारयेत् ।

(Nāślīlaṁ kīrtyet kancit pralāpam na ca kāryet)

— *Śukra Nitih (3-65)*

Abusive and obscene words or phrases, idle talk and boasting, which cause trouble and destruction should not be spoken. 'Pralapa' here means lose talk, which has no relevance, and do harm.

The above taboos are for all classes of people and for the society as a whole; such directives related to speaking and talking are so important as to deserve a suitable place amongst the 'human rights'. If one refrains from such utterances, he will be regarded as a gentleman. He will be liked, loved and respected by everyone. Abiding by such injunctions, one requires constant practice, which is not difficult.

How to Speak

It is not that the sages and teachers have only decried the words, phrases and type of language that ought not to be spoken. They have, with the same force, also deliberated upon how to speak, what sort of ideas and emotions should be expressed, what kind of facial expressions should appear on the face of the speaker and the other niceties. The positive injunction is:

> काले हितं मितं ब्रूयाद विसंवादि पेशलम्।
> पूर्वाभिभाषी सुमुखः सुशीलः करूणा मृदुः ।।
> (Kāle hitaṁ mitaṁ bruyād visamvādi peślam
> Purvābhibhāşi sumukhaḥ suśilaḥ karunā mṛduḥ)
>
> — *Śukra Nitih (3-12)*
>
> *One should speak at an appropriate occasion, relevantly, in soft and pleasing words. He should bear tender looks, loving and delightful expressions on the face and speak altruistically.*

The couplet (*śloka*) mentions most of the niceties of speaking. Speaking altruistically greatly contributes to the delivery of the speaker. If while speaking, one is conscious of the self, the flavour of the speech is lost. The speaker must be like a fountain of thoughts emerging out of the spoken matter. The countenance of the speaker is equally important. There ought to exist appropriate smile, which must be so natural as to ward off any artificiality. The choice of words is equally important as also their pitch and modulation, etc. One, who cares to imbibe such niceties of speaking, is known for his charming delivery. He is liked and respected by the audience.

Sukra's Views

Consolidating the points further, Śukra has said:

> जनस्याशयमालक्ष्य यो यथा परितुष्यति।
> तं तथैवानुवर्तेत पराराधन पण्डितः ।।
> (Janasāśayamālaksya yo yathā parituşyati
> Taṁ tathaivānu vartet pārādhan panditah)
>
> — *Śukra Nitih (3-15)*
>
> *The person well-versed in the art of pleasing others should first try to understand the feelings of others, and speak and behave with them the way they may feel happy.*

Who then does not want to please others and be popular? However, everything does not happen as per one's wishes. One who really makes efforts in this direction ought to ascertain the desire and expectation of the audience. On that basis, if he speaks with the niceties discussed above, he would be an effective speaker.

Advice from Mahabharata

The advice from *Mahabharata* is:

यस्तु सर्वमभिप्रेक्ष्य पूर्वमेवाभिभाषते।
स्मित पूर्वाभिभाषी च तस्य लोकः प्रसीदति।।
(Yastu sarvambhipreksya pūrvāmevabhibhāşte
Smit pūrvabhibhāşī ca tasya lokaḥ prasīdati)

— *Mahabharata Shanti Parva (84-6)*

One, who understands the expectation of the listeners, speaks smilingly to everybody is liked and loved by all.

Smile and sweet tone are the two important assets for a successful speaker as indicated in the above couplet. It is a common experience that even harsh and unpleasant phrases and language blunt their sharp edge, if conveyed in soft words with suitable smile. One speaking to everyone in pleasant words smilingly tends to win over even the adversaries, what to say of friends.

Spoken Words Full of Feeling

Another idea gets further reinforced thus:

वात्सल्यात्सर्वभूतेभ्यो वाचा श्रोत्र सुखा गिरः ।
परितापो पघातश्च पारुष्यं चात्र गर्हितम।।
(Vātsalayātsarvabhutebhyo vāçā śrotra sukhā giraḥ
Paritāpo padyātśca pāruşyam̐ cātra garhitam)

— *Mahabharata Shanti Parva (191-14)*

The spoken words should be full of feelings of love and compassion for all the living beings and sound pleasant to the listener. Causing pain or verbal injuries to others are censurable actions.

The efficacy of the soft and loving words full of compassion and tenderness has been commented upon as:

पशवोऽपि वशं यान्ति दानैश्च मृदु भाषणैः ।
(Paśvōapi vaśam̐ yānti dānaiśca mridu bhāśnaiḥ)

— *Śukra Nitih (3-86)*

Animals can also be controlled by feeding, love and calling soft words.

Such is the magic of soft words, feeling and sympathetic behaviour. If only this principle is adopted and practised, the humanity can come very close to divinity. This principle proves very effective and useful for managers as well. It has been generally observed that the managers, actually practising these principles have proved very effective and successful.

Qualities of a Good Speaker

Mahabharata has also provided the qualities that a good speaker and a learned person ought to possess. It has been provided as:

प्रवृत्तावाक्चित्रकथ ऊहवान प्रतिभानवान।
आशु ग्रन्थस्य वक्ता च यः स पण्डित उच्यते।।

(Pravŗttavakcittrakath uhvan pratibanvan,
Ashu granthsya vakta ca yaḥ sa pandit ucayte)

— *Mahabharata Udyog Parva (33-28)*

One who speaks fluently, talks in a charming manner, conveys his idea logically, is an intellectual and one who can tell the intent of any book quickly, is called a learned person.

The qualities described in the above *śloka* contribute towards making ones personality charming. Talking fluently is not an important attribute. Talking fluently in a captivating style is the real high quality. Listeners sit captivated to listen to such speaker. Such charming language is a proper blend of various qualities, like proper judgement of the desire of audience, fluent delivery, use of suitable and sympathetic language, speaking to emanate from the heart, soft and clear language, use of appropriate body language, no contradictions, no false promises, reasoned arguments, and a host of other qualities.

Another attribute in the couplet is '*Āśu granthsya vaktā*', which means so sharp an intellect that one should be able to understand and appreciate any written text quickly, '*Granthnsya*' does not mean book alone but also includes any written text. If a person has the capacity to quickly understand any text carefully, he will be an action-oriented person. Such persons are effective and are liked by all.

How to Reply

Speaking and talking are affected by multifaceted skills. They are very simple, yet are mostly not practised with the result that they cause serious problems for the speaker. The basic formula is:

प्रविचार्योत्तरं देयं सहसा न वदेत क्वचित।

(Prativicāryattraṁ deyam sahasā na vadyet kvacit)

— *Śukra Nitih (3-66)*

The reply must always be well thought out. No reply should be given suddenly at the spur of the moment.

This is a very high quality of wisdom not only for managers but also for everyone else. Inculcating this habit is very useful and practical too. Before speaking or replying, its consequence must be thoroughly considered. It has been observed, that in order to show off, most people give a prompt reply and then later feel that the task could not be accomplished, for the reasons that the reply was not properly considered. Therefore, the sagacity demands that before replying, all the aspects are properly considered. The other aspect is that if a reply is given immediately, it is considered that the problem was so simple. If a problem is placed and the listener says that let me think over, the problem poser feels that the matter is not so simple. Therefore, the practice and habit of giving a well-considered reply is always useful and practical.

It has been observed that when asked something, most people, instead of giving a proper reply, spend quite a time in introducing the subject and tire the listener; in the process sometimes, the main issue gets sidelined. However, a person who knows how to talk effectively and purposefully talks relevantly.

The formula in this context is:

कथानिरूपम् प्रतिवचनम्।

(Kathanirupam prati vaćanam)

— *Chanakya Nitih (329)*

Reply should be given strictly in accordance with the question.

One, who brings this formula in practice, is precise and effective. He conveys the real sense so effectively that the listener is able to appreciate the matter clearly. The advice is so practical that the problems get resolved easily. Some refer to this quality as 'economy in talking'. They are of the view that the more one talks, the greater are the chances of mistakes and complication.

Eminence of Speaking

Speaking has been dealt by many thinkers, scholars and sages in India that can easily convince anyone about the conclusion that the communication system in ancient India was so developed that the modern thinkers have not been able to contribute any original thought or theory worth the name. Therefore, it may be relevant to study the thoughts of another ancient sage and poet, who not only imparted knowledge about communication but was also a behavioural scientist of great repute. This poet sage is Valmiki, the composer of the epic *Ramayana*. This ancient epic reveals the deep insight of Valmiki into the principles of communication through his portrayal of Hanuman as an excellent speaker.

Valmiki's Contribution

Hanuman's first conversation was with Sri Ram, as an emissary of Sugrīva, the younger brother of the King Bali of Kiśkindha. Hanuman was sent by Sugrīva on the mission to explore if Sri Ram and Lakśman were the agents of Bali with any design to kill Sugrīva. It was a difficult mission. However, Hanuman with his proficiency and wisdom could correctly perceive the reason why Sri Ram was there. He correctly estimated their strength and persuaded them to be friendly with Sugrīva. Such accomplishments are directly attributable to the excellence of Hanuman's speaking abilities.

Appreciating the brilliance of Hanuman,s speaking aptitude, Valmiki has used adorned him with the phrases, like *'Vak Kushal'*, *'Vak Vishard'*, *'Subhāshitam'*, which are all superlatives.

Hanuman's Speaking Faculties

In the first ever meeting, the style adopted by Hanuman was:

ततः स हनुमान वाचां श्लक्षणया सुमनोज्ञया ।
विनीत वदुपागम्य राघवौ प्रणिपत्य च ।।
(Tataḥ sa Hanumān vāchāḿ ślakṣanyā sumojňyā
vinīt vadupāgamya Rāghvo pŕanipatya ca)

— *Ramayana Kiśkindha Kand (3-34)*

Hanuman approached Sri Ram and Lakśman and started praising them with soft and loving words.

After enquiring as to who they were, he enquired about their purpose of coming to such a dense and dangerous forest full of difficulties and wildlife. Thereafter, he narrated his own perception about them. He said that they appeared to be princes and highest class of warriors.

When, even on being asked, the two brothers kept silent, Hanuman politely questioned the silence. He in turn disclosed his own identity and purpose, after which he kept quiet.

Sri Ram's Perception

It was at this stage that Sri Ram advised Lakśman to speak to Hanuman but wisely, since Hanuman was no ordinary person as was evident from his mannerisms and style of speaking. These qualities are narrated in *Ramayana* one by one.

Sri Ram said to Lakśman that the way Hanuman spoke was not possible, unless the person had studied *Sam Veda*, *Rig Veda* and *Yajur Veda*. It was evident by his speech that he had studied and learnt grammar. This was so for the obvious reason that Hanuman did not utter even a single faulty word.

Valmiki's Deep Insight

Sri Ram, while narrating the qualities of Hamuman, further says:

> न मुखे नेत्रेयोर्वाऽपि ललाटे भ्रुवोस्तथा ।
> अन्येष्वपि च ग्रात्रेषु दोषः संविदितः क्वचित् । ।
> (Na mukhe netreryorvapi lalāte bhruvostatha
> Aneyşvapi ca gātreşu dośḥ saḿviditah kvachit)
>
> — *Ramayana Kiśkindha Kand (3-30)*

While speaking, his (Hanuman's) face, eyes, forehead, eyebrows or any other part of the body did not exhibit any distortion or disharmony with the spoken words or ideas.

A perfect harmony between the spoken word and the idea expressed is a great quality. The above *śloka* bears the testimony of Valmiki's deep insight into the science of communication. He exhibits complete knowledge of the efficacy of matching facial expressions and body language with the spoken words.

In yet another *śloka*, Valmiki has clearly indicated when and to what extent to speak, the tone, the pitch, the modulation etc. He has said:

अविस्तरम संदिग्धमविलम्बितमद्रुतम ।
उरः स्थं कण्ठगं वाक्यं वर्तते मध्यमे स्वरे । ।
(Avistaraṁ sandigdham vilambitmadrutam
Uraḥsthaṁ kanthgam vakyam vartake madhyame svare)
— *Ramayana Kiśkindha Kand (3-31)*

He (Hanuman) neither extended his talking to the extent that the listener gets bored nor made it so short and precise as to create confusion. While talking, he neither delayed his delivery nor hurried about it. His utterances were coming from the heart and had no artificiality. He said the most appropriate words where they ought to have been said and in soft tone and pitch.

Sri Ram further said:

संस्कार क्रम सम्पन्नामद्रुताम विलम्बिताम ।
उच्चारयति कल्याणीं वाचं हृदयहारिणम । ।
अनया चित्रया वाचा त्रिस्थानव्यंजनस्थया ।
कस्य नाराध्यते चित्तमुधयतासेररेरपि । ।
(Sanskār kram sampannāmadrutām vilambitām
Uccārayati kalyānim vācaṁ hriday hārinam
Anyā citrayā vācā tristhānavyaṁjansthyā
kasya nārādhyte cittamudyatā serarerapi)
— *Ramayana Kiśkindha Kand (3-32, 33)*

His (Hanuman's) speaking had a perfect conditioning of the grammar, purposeful, relevant and fluent. His delivery was neither too high nor too low. It was full of softness and all other good qualities. His voice coming out of his heart, mind and throat was so sweet and pleasant that it could even move and deter an enemy who was about to attack, what to say of others.

Further, appreciating the excellence of Hanuman's abilities, Sri Ram said to Lakśman:

एवं गुणगणैर्युक्ता यस्य स्युः कार्यसाधकाः ।
तस्य सिध्यन्ति सर्वार्था दूत वाक्य प्रचोदिताः । ।
(Evam gunaganairyuktā yasya syuḥ kāryasādhakāh
Tasya siddhyanti sarvārtha dūt vākya pracaoditah)
The King who has such an able and successful emissary can fulfil all his aims and achieve success.

Laksman's Perception

On the advice of Sri Ram, Lakśman talked to Hanuman and concluded his views thus:

प्रसन्न मुख वर्णश्च व्यक्तं हृष्टश्च भाषते।
नानृतं वक्षयते धीरो हनुमान मारुतात्मजः ।।
(Prasanna mukh varnaśca vyaktam hŗştaśca bhāşte
Nānritaṁ vakşyate dhiro Hanumān mārutāmjah)
— *Ramayana Kiśkindha Kand (4-32)*

The manner, in which Hanuman was talking pleasantly and cheerfully, was indicative that he never speaks lies.

Such is the result of excellence in talking that a person in the first ever conversation perceives the talker as perfectly truthful. Such person is worth being called as successful, effective and a perfect speaker and that Hanuman was as perceived and identified by the Sage Valmiki.

Secrets of Hanuman's Speaking Talent

The secret of Hanuman's success in speaking, as described by Valmiki, was his unshaken faith in certain virtues of high order that Hanuman always believed and lived.

After being installed as the King of Kiśkindha, Sugrīva got involved in leading a sensuous life. He forgot the promise he made to Sri Ram that after the end of the rainy season, he would send search parties to locate Sita. Directed by Sri Ram, Lakśman came to Kiśkindha in fury. It was at such time that Hanuman spoke to inspire Sugrīva not to forget the promise given to Sri Ram. The words in which he spoke to his King Sugrīva have been described thus:

हितं तत्वं च पथ्यं च समधर्मार्थ नितिमत।
प्रणयप्रीतिसंयुक्तम विश्वास कृत निश्चयम।।
(Hitam tatavam ca pathyam ca samdarmarthanitimat
Pranayapritisamyuktam visvaskrit niscayam)
— *Ramayana Kiśkindha Kand (13-8)*

He spoke to Sugrīva in truthful, beneficial, appeasing, propitiating, dutiful, welfare-oriented, loving, affectionate and reliable words, on which he (Hanuman) himself had faith.

Conclusion

Hanuman has been described by Valmiki as '*sarvaśastra vid*', the one having deep insight into all branches of knowledge. This is based on no wishful thinking or reverence alone. This statement emerges true if the deeds of Hanuman are analysed. He excels as a warrior, a commander, a dedicated missionary, an emissary, an advisor, a friend, a sagacious person, a counsellor, a protector, a behavioural scientist, selfless, truthful, and a repository of wisdom. There is a lot to learn from this mighty character.

The foregoing description sufficiently proves that the communication system, which gives a deceptive look of being modern, was fully developed and was the forerunner of most of the modern thoughts and theories.

○○

10

Manage Your Writing (Management of Written Communication)

Communication Discussed

Managers spend more time in communicating than in any other activity. They have to ensure that the messages pass on without distortion or misunderstanding. Their emphasis should be on making their communication short and precise, yet clear, focused and to-the-point.

Communication connotes any method that one employs to convey his ideas, emotions, imaginations and experience to any other person or persons to meet the objective. It is sharing of goal-oriented messages between two or more persons through a medium or media.

The medium or media may be verbal or non-verbal. While the verbal must be articulate, the non-verbal may generally be silent, gestures, eyes, body language and writing. It is the writing, which makes a man precise and exact.

Some Indian teachers, thinkers, scholars and sages of the ancient period have made significant contributions to the verbal and non-verbal media of communication.

Beginning of Writing

In ancient India, listening (*śruti*) and remembering (*smriti*) were the two modes of learning. Then came in the writing as a necessity. It has been said:

अनुभूत स्मारकं तु लिखितं ब्रह्मण कृतम् ।

(Anubhūt smārkam tu likhitaṁ brahamana kṛtam)

— *Śukra Nitih (4-5-169)*

Brahma, the creator, brought the writing into being for the people to retain the memory of the experienced matter.

The hidden meaning is that writing perpetuates further thinking and the cycle goes on and on. However, writing is a skill that can be acquired and developed by constant learning and practice.

Indian Thinkers

The great thinkers, scholars and teachers of ancient India have exhibited original thinking on written communication. Being foresighted teachers, they have adopted practical approach.

Indian sages have not lost sight of even the minutest important matter. Writer is an important person both in the state and society. In the context of the law courts, Śukra has prescribed that the writer must write exactly what has been said. He further describes the qualities of a writer as:

गणना कुशलो यस्तु देशभाषाप्रभेदवित् ।
असन्दिग्धमगूढर्थं विलिखेत्स च लेखकः ।।

(Ganana kuślo yastu deśabhaṣa prabhedvit
Asandigdhamguḍhartham vilikhetsa ca lekhkaḥ)

— *Śukra Nitih (3-174)*

The writer should be proficient in calculations, should be well conversant with the variations of the nation's languages, doubtless, capable of understanding the meaning and writing clearly and legibly.

A writer ought to possess thorough knowledge of the language, unless he has this quality, it may not be possible for him to convey the sense properly. Sir Francis Bacon has remarked, "Reading maketh a full man, conference a ready man and writing an exact man."

In that view of Bacon, if the writer is not clear about his concepts, he will not be an effective writer. This is what Śukra and Kautilya have emphasised in the ancient period.

Kautilya has classified all the written matters into thirteen groups. Then he mentions that the written documents are of seven types.

There are six attributes of excellent writing and five kinds of defects. Each point has been lucidly explained with examples and nothing has been left for guesswork.

Matters Arising out of Writing

Kautilya has enumerated thirteen matters that may arise out of writing. These have been clubbed as:

निन्दा प्रशंसा पृच्छा च तथाख्यानमथार्थना।
प्रत्याख्यानमुपालम्भः प्रतिषेधोऽथ चोदना।।
सांत्वमभ्युपपत्तिश्च भर्त्सनानुनयौ तथा।
एतेष्वर्थाः प्रवर्तन्ते त्रयोदशसु लेखजाः।।
(Nindā praśansā pricchā ca tathā khyanmthārthnā
Pratyā khyanamupolambhaḥ pratiṣedhotha cōdanā
Sāntvamabhuppattśca bhartsnānunyau tathā
Eteṣvarthāḥ pravartante trayodaśasu lekhjāḥ)

— *Artha Śastra (2-10-23, 24)*

Censure, praise, query, statement, request, refusal, reproof, prohibition, injunction, appeasement, help, threatening and propitiation are the thirteen matters arising out of the writing concerned.

This list of the thirteen matters, at first sight, appears to be short, but in fact, it is so comprehensive that hardly any matter is left out. Almost all types of written communication get included in one or the other category. The thirteen types have not only been enumerated but each one of them has been explained with sufficient clarity and precision along with examples as:

1. Censure

तत्रभिजन शरीर कर्मणा दोष वचनं निन्दा।
(Tatrabhijan śarira karmana doṣa vacanaṁ ninda)

— *Artha Śastra (2-10-26)*

Mention of defects concerning birth, body or action is 'censure'.

Any mention of defects concerning the action provides a wide scope to the definition. In the present context, defect in action is censurable. Besides, the defects concerning birth include 'low-born' (नीच जाति), 'one-legged' (लंगड़ा) 'One-eyed' (काणा), etc.

2. Praise

गुणवचन मे तेषामेव प्रशंसा । ।

(Gunavacan me teṣāmeva praśansā)

— Artha Śastra (2-10-26)

Mention of merits is praise. It may pertain to good qualities, deeds, actions, doings and so on.

Verbal praise boosts up the morale but fades out with the passage of time. Any written appreciation has a long lasting effect. A written appreciation is often considered as a reward and encouragement to the employee. Many a times, the recorded praise helps in the long run. Praise in the form of appreciation acts as an index of the person's brightness.

3. Query

कथमेतद इति पृच्छा ।

(Kathametad iti pṛccha)

— Artha Śastra (2-10-27)

'How is this so?' is a query.

It is in the form of a question, an enquiry and helps in removing doubts, leading to better understanding. Many a times, a query is raised to collect more information regarding an issue or to clear confusions.

4. Statement

एवम् इत्याख्यानम् ।

(Evam ityākhyānam)

— Artha Śastra (2-10-28)

'Thus, it so...' is a statement.

Narration of facts, any incident, occurrence, information, disclosure, and happenings are all statements. Most of the part of writing can be classified as statement.

5. Request

देहि इत्यर्थना ।

(Dehi ityrthnā)

— Artha Śastra (2-10-29)

'Give it to me' is a request. The basic ingredient of request shall be 'dehi'.

Seeking favour or support, asking for some money or things are included in request. Sometimes requests are made in direct form, like 'please give me some money'. Many a times, things are asked in a refined and indirect form. There is a suitable phrase in Urdu language called '*Husne talab*' (*हुस्न-ए-तलब*), meaning the beauty of asking. For example, suppose one has gone to a friend who has asked his servant to bring the tea. But the visitor wants coffee instead. So he says to the friend, 'I have a sweet memory of the wonderful coffee being prepared in your house'. Now the host understands and sends for coffee instead of tea. This is known as the beauty of asking. Such asking also comes within the scope of 'request'.

6. Refusal

न प्रयच्छामि इति प्रत्याख्यानम् ।

(Na pryacchāmi iti pratyākhānam)

—Artha Śastra (2-10-30)

'I will not give' is refusal.

Refusal is connected with request. The explanation given above depicts only an example. Refusal will have as many forms as request. In short, not granting a request amounts to refusal. However, it can be used independently as well. For example, one may show some good books to a friend and may say that I never give my books to anyone. This also amounts to refusal.

7. Reproof

अननुरूपं भवतः इत्युपालम्भः ।

(Ananurupaṁ bhavataḥ itupalambhaḥ)

—Artha Śastra (2-10-31)

'This is unworthy of you' is a reproof or reprimand.

Reprimands can be verbal as well as written. It is like rebuke, shame, disgrace or censure. It is a shade more serious than censure. When one does not improve even after censure, reprimand is issued. If it is in writing, it aims at deterring repetition of certain acts.

8. Prohibition

मा कार्षी इति प्रतिषेधः ।

(Mā kārṣi iti pratiṣedhaḥ)

—Artha Śastra (2-10-32)

'This is not to be done' is prohibition.

In the days of Kautilya, the courts as well as the administrators could issue the decree of prohibition. In modern times as well, the same procedure continues with the addition that a writ of prohibition can also be issued as a constitutional measure. In so far as a classification of writing is concerned, an advice from one to the other can also fall under this class.

9. Injunction

इदम् क्रियताम इति चोदना ।

(Idam kriyatam iti cōdana)

— *Artha Śastra (2-10-33)*

'Let this be done' is an injunction.

Such orders could be issued by the courts or the administrative authorities through written and sometimes verbal communications. Though, it has been described as an old practice, but it continues even today in the same form.

10. Appeasement

योऽहं स भवान यंममं द्रव्यं तम्दवतः इत्युपग्रहः सान्त्वतम ।

(Yoahaṁ sa bhavān yammam dravaṁ tadbhavaḥ itupgraḥ sāntvatam)

— *Artha Śastra (2-10-34)*

'What am I is you, what objects belong to me are yours' such conciliation is appeasement.

The four *upāyās* (strategies) of winning people have already been discussed in a separate chapter. This is the first of the said four strategies, the *sam.*

11. Help

व्यसन साहाय्यमभ्युपपत्तिः ।

(Vyasan sahayyambhupapattiḥ)

— *Artha Śastra (2-10-35)*

'Aid or assistance provided in calamity' is help.

However, help is limited not only to calamities, as it is also rendered or provided on various considerations. This is a very effective medium of winning people.

12. Threatening

सदोषमायति प्रदर्शनमभिभर्त्सनम् ।

(Sadoşmāyāti pradaśnmbhibhartsnam)

— *Artha Śastra (2-10-36)*

'I will see you' is threatening, which represents a future full of danger.

This is a situation in which a person warns the other one of dire consequences. Written threatening takes many forms. Some communication conveys directions, disobedience of which is said to be seriously viewed.

Many a times, employees are warned to be careful in future, otherwise disciplinary action could be taken. In such cases, the fact remains that the authority issuing the communication possesses full competence to take the action, even if the same is not included in the warning. In such cases, the threat of disciplinary action is useless. On the other hand, the threatening looks like brandishing the sword for nothing. The managers ought to take care of such situation as it is a matter of projection of one's own image.

13. Propitiation

अनुनयस्त्रिविधोऽर्थ कृतावतिक्रमे पुरुषा दिव्यसने चेति ।

(Anunayastrivirdhoarth kŗāvatikrame puruşā
divyasane ceti)

— *Artha Śastra (2-10-37)*

Propitiation (appeasement or to render some favour) may be threefold; in doing a thing, in case of transgression (passing beyond a limit) and during calamity of a person.

Appeasement is done to render some favour in one way or the other, which includes sacrifice too. One may directly do a favour or may put a check on the other who may be trying to cross the limits. It can also be done to help out someone in difficulty.

Thus, Kautilya has precisely classified all the written matters into thirteen categories. Such classification has been done by other sages as well. For example, Śukra has enumerated as many as nineteen types of writing and has described their characteristics. Yet, Kautilya's approach is more precise and practical.

Kinds of Documents — Decrees

After highlighting the thirteen categories of written matters, Kautilya proceeds to classify the written documents, which according to him are of eight types. Enumerating them, he says:

> प्रज्ञापनाज्ञा परिदान लेखास्तथा परिहार निसृष्ट लेखौ।
> प्रवृत्तिकश्च प्रतिलेख एव सर्वत्रगश्चेति हि शासनानि।।
> (Prajñāpanajñā paridānlekhāstathā parihār nisrişta lekhau
> Pravŗttikśca pratilekh eva sarvatragataśceti he śāsnāni)
>
> *— Artha Śastra (2-10-38)*
>
> *Documents of communication, command, gift, exemption, authorisation, giving news of a happening, reply and those applicable everywhere are the various types of decrees.*

Though Kautilya has separately described the thirteen matters that may arise of writing and eight types of written decrees, Śukra has enumerated nineteen varieties of written documents, which included both the types described separately by Kautilya. While Śukra has shown the tendency of mixing the issues; Kautilya's approach is more analytical and precise. He mostly behaves like a teacher. After naming the kinds of decrees, he proceeds to explain each one.

1. Communication (Prajñā)

> अनेन विज्ञापितमेवमाह तद्दीयतां चेघदि तत्त्वमस्ति।
> राज्ञः समीपे वरकारमाह प्रज्ञापनैषा विविधोपदिष्टा।।
> (Anen vijñāpitmevamāh Tddiytāṁ cedydi tatvmasti
> Rājñaḥ samipe varkārmāh Prajñāpanaişā vividhopdişta)
>
> *— Artha Śastra (2-10-39)*
>
> *Two types of communication have been shown here. One is that, "You are reported to be having a horse worthy of the King. If that is true, give it to the King. " The second is, "I have learnt that the King has approved your action, you will certainly get some benefit". These are decrees of communication.*

When some information from an authority is passed by one person to the other on the basis of knowledge gained about it, that is known as a document or decree of communication. For example, it is written, "So and so have spoken of an excellent deed in the presence of the boss". Such documents of communication may be of different kinds.

♣

2. Command (आज्ञा-Ājñā)

भर्तुराज्ञा भवेद्यत्र निग्रहानुग्रहौ प्रति।
विशेषेण तु भृत्येषु तदाज्ञालेखलक्षणम्।।
(Bharturajñā bhavedyatra nigrhānugrhau prati
Viśeşen tu bhŗtyeşu tadājnālakh lakşnam)

— Artha Śastra (2-10-40)

Where there is a command of the King, administrator or the court regarding punishment, reward or favour, especially in the matter of employees, that is the characteristic of a decree of command.

The basic ingredient of this type of decree is the command (आज्ञा) of the competent authority. It ought to be an order, neither an advice nor a recommendation.

3. Favour or Gift (परिदान — Paridān)

यथार्हगुणसंयुक्ता पूजा यत्रोपलक्ष्यते।
अप्याधौ परिदाने वा भवतस्तावुपग्रहौ।।
(Arthārhgunsanyuktā pujā yatroplakşyte
Apyādhau paridāne vā bharvatastāvupagrahau)

— Artha Śastra (2-10-41)

Where honour is rendered in accordance with merit or gift is given as a reward or help in distress, the document concerned is known as a decree of favour or gift.

4. Exemption (परिहार — Parihar)

जाते विशेषेषु पुरेषु चैव ग्रामेषु देशेषु चतेषु तेषु।
अनुग्रहो यो नृपतेर्निदेशा तिज्ज्ञः परिहार इति व्यवस्येत।।
(Jāte viśeşeșu pureșu caaiva gŕāmeşu deśşu ca teşu teşu
Anugŗaho yo nripaternideşā tijajnaḥ parihār iti vyavsyet)

— Artha Śastra (2-10-42)

The favour, which is conferred at the command of the King or the authority on various castes and on different cities, villages and regions, is called as the decree of exemption.

Such exemption mainly means exemption from taxes. Exemption to some castes and people prevail even these days and so also exemption to village and regions. For example at the time of natural calamities, certain villages and regions are granted exemption from payments of land revenue and interest free loans by the Government.

5. Authority or Delegation of Authority (निसृष्टि—Nisrsti)

निसृष्टि स्थापना कार्य करणे वचने तथा।
एष वाचिक लेखः स्याद भवेनै सृष्टिकोऽपि वा।
(Nisŗşti sthāpanā kārya karane vacane tathā
Eşa vācik lekhaḥ syād bhavenai sŗşti koapi vā)

Artha Śastra (2-10-43)

Possession or delegation of authority for doing a work and in the matter of issuing orders, this may be a document authorising the issue of orders or containing an authorisation for doing a work.

In view of decentralisation, delegation of authority is at the core. However, delegation of authority has its roots into the Vedic period, which continued through the Kautilyan period to the modern days as well.

6. Happening (प्रवृत्तिं — Pravrittim)

विविधां दैव संयुक्ता तत्वजां चैव मानुषीम्।
द्विविधां तां व्यवस्यान्ति प्रवृत्तिं शासनं प्रति।।
(Vividhāṁ daiva sanyuktā tatvajāṁ caaiva mānuşim
Dvividhām tāṁ vyvasyānti pravŗttim śāsanaṁ prati)

— Artha Śastra (2-10-44)

The document describing a happening may be of two types. The one associated with Divine and the other concerning human beings. Based on facts, happenings may of several varieties, but can be classified into two types stated above.

7. Document in Reply (प्रतिलेख — Pratilekh)

दृष्ट्वा लेखं यथातत्वं ततः प्रत्यनुभाष्य च।
प्रतिलेखो भवेत्कार्यो यथा राजवचस्तथा।।
(Dŗştvā lekhaṁ yathātatvaṁ tataḥ pratynubhāsyaca
Pratilekho bhavetkāryo yathā rājvacasthā)

— Artha Śastra (2-10-45)

After fully examining the document as it really is and then closely reading it, the document in reply should be prepared. It should be exactly in accordance with the royal ruling.

The words 'yatha rajvacastatha' means 'exactly as the words of the King may be' are significant enough.

If the word 'authority' is substituted for the 'King', the directive becomes applicable to modern times. The directive is that full care of any possible distortion must be taken. The exact words of the authority that dictates the reply have to be strictly adhered to and followed, only then it takes the shape of a document in reply.

8. Decree Applicable Everywhere (सर्वत्रगतश्चेति — Sarvatra gataśceti)

यत्रेश्वरांश्चाधिकृतांश्च राजा रक्षोपकारौ पथिकार्थमाह।
सर्वत्रगो नाम भवेत्स मार्गे देशे च सर्वत्र च वेदितव्यः।।
(Ytreśvarnścādhkriśca Raja Pakşpakārau pathi kārth māh
Sarbatrago nām bhavetsa marge deśe ca sarvatra
ca veditavaḥ)

— *Artha Śastra (2-10-46)*

The directions by which the King or the authority asks the officers to ensure protection and comforts for travellers and others, would be the decree applicable everywhere. For example, army being called to meet the flood situation, etc.

Attributes of Excellence in Writing

After describing in detail the various kinds of documents and decrees, Kautilya proceeds to explain the attributes of excellent writing. He enumerates six characteristics in a couplet (*śloka*). Thereafter, he explains each quality one by one. The said six qualities are:

अर्थक्रम संबंधः परिपूर्णता माधुर्यमौदार्यं।
स्पष्टत्वमिति लेखं संपत्।।
(Arthakrama sambandhaḥ paripurnta
Madhuryamauduryaṁ spaşt tvamiti lekh sampat)

— *Artha Śastra (2-10-6)*

The arrangement of subject matter, connection, completeness, sweetness, exaltedness and lucidity constitute the excellence of writing.

All these qualities of writing should remain constantly and perpetually. But arranging them in a proper and workable order is the prime art, which Kautilya possessed in abundance. He has explained each quality thus:

1. **Arrangement of Subject Matter (*अर्थक्रमः* — Artha Kramaḥ)**

तत्र यथावदनुपूर्वक्रया प्रधानस्यार्थस्य ।
पूर्वमभिनिवेश इत्यर्थक्रमः । ।
(Tatra yathavadnupurva kŗya pranasyarthsya
Purvambhiniveś itythkramaḥ)

— *Artha Śastra (2-10-7)*

Arrangement of the matter in proper order is the the principal quality of a good document. The directive that the matter be presented in a proper order still continues to be followed. The practice is that the principal matter, or the subject, is written at the top of a communication. This makes the reader aware of what the letter is about and thus helps him in understanding the matter that follows. If the subject matter is not stated, the contents of the communication may be confusing or interpreted differently. Not indicating the subject matter in the beginning constitutes a defective writing.

2. **Connection (*संबंधः* — Sambandhaḥ)**

प्रस्तुतस्यार्थस्यानुपरोधा दुत्तरस्य विधानभा
समाप्रेरिति संबंधः ।
(Prastutsyārthasyānuprodhā duttarasya vidhānabhā
samāpreriti sambandhaḥ)

— *Artha Śastra (2-10-8)*

Presentation of the subject matter should be compatible with the matter in hand right up to the end. This attribute has been defined as 'connection'.

The matter in the communication should be connected with the subject matter throughout. Such quality obviates the chances of any divergence. It will also make the communication short, precise, to-the-point and focused.

3. **Completeness (*परिपूर्णता* — Paripūrntā)**

अर्थपदाक्षराणां मन्यूनति रिक्तता हेतुदाहरण
दृष्टन्तैरर्थोपवर्णन श्रान्त पदतेति परिपूर्णता ।
(Arthpadākşranāṁ manyunati riktatā hetudāhrana
drştntairarthorpavarnan śrāntpadteti paripurntā)

— *Artha Śastra (2-10-8)*

There should be no deficiency in expression. There should be no excess matter or words or letters, unnecessary description of details, reasons, citations and illustrations. Such comprehensive expressiveness has been named as 'completeness'.

The matter or the material contained in the communication ought to be relevant and concise. Only necessary details should be given. The matter should be supported by appropriate reasons and details. Only such phrases should be used which adhere to the intent and purpose of the communication. Thus, almost all the merits of written communication find place in this quality, completeness. Yet that is not all. The teacher goes further, describing the other attributes of a good written communication in the *ślokas* to come.

4. Sweetness (माधुर्यम् — Mādhuryam)

सुखोपनीत चार्वर्थशब्दाभिधानं माधुर्यम् ।

(Sukhopanit cārvarthaśabdabhidanam madhuryam)

— *Artha Śastra (2-10-10)*

Selection and usage of pleasant words constitute the quality 'sweetness'.

The words used in writing should be pleasant, easy to understand and also appropriate. Such charm and sweetness may be possible, if the person writing or dictating the communication is peaceful, relaxed, tension-free and is aware of the exact purpose of writing. He must be considerate and reasonable.

Use of sweet words and expressions in the *sam* strategy has the effect of winning over the people. Conciliatory approach is much effective as compared to the threatening one. A person in authority should never write to a wrong doing person using harsh expressions, such as 'severe action will be taken for disobedience of orders'. Such a written threat is superfluous for the one who possesses the authority. Even if this had not been written, the authority could take action. So what is the point in writing such language? The authority, could better write that it was hoped and believed that he would improve and would not repeat the same mistakes. Sweet language has its own magic.

5. Exaltedness (औदार्य — Audāryam)

अग्राम्य शब्दाभिधानमौदार्यम् ।

(Agrāmya śabdābhidhānmaudāryam)

— *Artha Śastra (2-10-11)*

Use of the words that are not vulgar is exaltedness. Any written communication must contain refined words, avoiding the base ones.

Using base words or unrefined phrases, abusive expressions cause double harm. In the first place, it spoils the taste of the communication, which is not appreciated, and secondly, the personality and the taste of the writer fall in disrepute.

6. Lucidity (स्पष्टत्वमिति — Spastatvamiti)

प्रतीत शब्द प्रयोगः स्पष्टत्वमिति ।

(Pratit śabda prayogah spaṣṭatvamiti)

— *Artha Śastra (2-10-11)*

Use of easy and familiar words is lucidity. The words 'Pratit śabda' are the key words in this definition. 'Pratit' is used to denote well-known.

Lucidity is the resultant effect when familiar words, phrases and expressions are used. This practice avoids confusion, brings clarity and makes the communication correctly understood and interpreted.

There are some writings, which are difficult to be understood by an average reader without consulting a dictionary. For example, use of the word 'aqua' in place of water is opposed to the principle of lucidity.

The six points that we have discussed denote the excellence of writing. Yet if the defects of writing are also known, their antithesis may add to the list of good writing.

Defects of Writing

Kautilya has cautioned against the defects in writing (*lekh dośaḥ*). He has described five such defects. First he has enumerated all the defects in one śloka, and then, he has dealt with each one of them separately in detail. The five defects of writing are:

अकान्तिर्व्याघातः पुनरुक्तमपशब्दः संपल्वः इतिलेख दोषाः ।

(Akāntirvyāghātaḥ punruktampaśabdḥ samplvaḥ
iti lekh doṣaḥ)

— *Artha Śastra (2-10-57)*

Absence of charm, contradiction, repetition, incorrect use of words and confusion are the five defects of writing.

In the real spirit of a teacher, Kautilya does not leave the enumeration of defects as they are. Thereafter, he has given proper examples to explain each defect.

1. **Absence of Charm (अकान्ति — Akānti)**

तत्र कालपत्रकचारु विषयम विरागाक्षरत्वम अकान्तिः ।

(Tatra kālpatrakcāru viṣyam viragakṣratvam akantiḥ)

— *Artha Śastra (2-10-58)*

Among the defects of writing, the use of black leaf (bad paper), writing unattractive, uneven and faint letters constitute the absence of charm.

Here, the use of black leaf has been mentioned because in Kautilyan period, most writing was done on leaves and thin bark of trees called '*tamal patra*'. In the present context this may be substituted by deep coloured, torn and dirty paper.

In written communication, much depends upon the paper, handwriting, lines, ink and pen used and impression of the letters. If the paper is good, the handwriting too tends to be attractive. Nobody wants to read something written in bad hand and on a dirty or waste paper.

2. **Contradiction (व्याघात — Vyaghat)**

पूर्वेण पश्चिमस्या नुपपत्ति व्याघातः ।

(Purvena paścimasyā nupapati vyāghātaḥ)

— *Artha Śastra (2-10-59)*

Incompatibility of the later with the earlier or vice-versa constitutes contradiction.

This defect, many a times comes up inadvertently. If the writer is not fully attentive, he may, at some stage, contradict his own earlier statement. For example, a senior officer recorded an adverse remark in the confidential report of his subordinate officer, "He is a short-tempered person, but maintains poise at the time of pressure of work." This remark has a built-in contradiction.

3. **Repetition (पुनरुक्तम — Punaruktam)**

उक्तस्या विशेषण द्वितीयमुच्चारणं पुनरुक्तम ।

(Uktasya vissen dvitiyamuccaranam punruktam)

— *Artha Śastra (2-10-60)*

A recurrence of what has already been said, without any distinction is repetition.

This is the most common ailment of a written communication. Ineffective writers make monotonous repetition of 'ands' and 'buts'. Use of 'however', 'moreover', 'nevertheless', etc used to introduce a sentence are not known to them. They also fail to substitute a commonplace word like 'brave' by its near synonyms, like courageous, fearless, dauntless etc. Such clichés kill the beauty of the writing and make it monotonous.

4. Incorrect Use of a World (अपशब्दः —Apaśabdah)

लिंग वचन कालकारकाणामन्यथा प्रयोगोपऽपशब्दः ।

(Ling vaćan kālkārkānāmanythā prayogoap śabdaḥ)

— Artha Śastra (2-10-61)

Wrong use of gender, number, tense and case are all incorrect use of words.

Such defects creep in inadvertently for many reasons. For example, in Hindi, the word '*anek*' (vusd) means 'many' which is plural in itself; yet, many use the word '*anekon*' (vusdks) as plural.

When a person writes in a different language, such defects sometimes come up. For example, a Bengali writing '*kyā āp āyegā*' instead of '*kyā āp āyenge*' or '*ham chai khaya*' for '*hamne chai pī*'.

In an interesting example, an officer writing the confidential report of his subordinate wrote 'he hardly works' when he wanted to write 'he is a hard worker'.

5. Confusion (संप्लवः — Samplavaḥ)

अवर्गे वर्गकरणं वर्गे चा वर्ग कृया गुणविपर्यास संप्लवः ।

(Avarge vargakrnamí varge cā varg kṛiyā gunaviparyās samplavaḥ)

— Artha Śastra (2-10-62)

Making of combinations where it should not be and not making where it should be creates confusion. For example, 'Government as G.O.', 'C.I.D. Department', 'where some adverse reports are received we shall order re-poll once again' etc.

Summing Up

Kautilya considered a written communication so important that he prescribed the King's (administrator's) writer to possess the qualities of a minister and be conversant with the conventions. He should also have a good handwriting, be capable of reading, understanding and appreciative of any document in its true perspective. He should also be quick in composing.

While sitting with the King (substitute it with administrator), the writer should listen attentively. He should reduce the matter in writing in an attractive hand and pleasing language. Kautilya has said that he has written so much about the qualities of writings for the benefit of the writers and scribes.

The thinkers and scholars preceding Kautilya had not written on the scribes. The Kautilyan work is based on his original thoughts. He has written so much after careful and detailed study of all *śastras* and sciences as well as the practices prevailing. Such work coming from Kautilya is unparalleled for the reason that he was deeply involved in statecraft. Though, the Kautilyan work was written in the ancient period, around 320 B.C., yet the thoughts propounded by him are quite relevant for the modern period. This chapter would benefit all those who really want to gain knowledge from the directives of the great thinkers, scholars, philosophers, politicians and teachers of India. One must know that everything can be learnt from the great heritage of this country.

This chapter on the knowledge about written communication does not seem to be complete unless the thought of Kautilya about concluding a piece of writing gets exposure. He has said:

लेख परिसंहरणार्थ इति शब्दो वाचिकमस्येति च।

(Lekh parisamharanartha iti śabdo vacikmasyetica)

— *Artha Śastra (2-10-22)*

For concluding the writing, the word 'iti' (इति) and 'these are the words of so and so' should be used.

So, the writing of this chapter is mainly based on Kautilya's *Artha Śastra. Iti shri* (*shri* is my addition)!

○○

11

Discipline

Discipline Explained

Man-management largely depends upon discipline, which basically is a positive connotation. In Sanskrit, the word '*vinayaḥ*' (विनयः) means discipline, direction, injunction and moral teaching. In English, discipline is a derivative of disciple, which means learner.

Discipline has been sufficiently deliberated upon by ancient Indian thinkers, sages and scholars. It has been classified by Kautilya thus:

कृतकः स्वाभाविकश्च विनयः ।
(Kṛtakaḥ svābhāvikśca vinayaḥ)

— *Artha Śastra (1-5-3)*

Discipline is twofold acquired and inborn.

It is conspicuous that there is no third category. So, imposed discipline has no place to perch upon. Child is born with some traits, the rest are acquired. The acquired discipline clusters around the in-born ones. This may be called the process of generation.

But what is that which we call discipline. For brevity sake, abiding by the socially accepted norms is defined as discipline. It can be used in various contexts, e.g. behaviour, work, way of life, and so on. Discipline has its impact on various functions of life, like playing, speaking, writing, thinking, management and a host of others. Each activity is guided by norms, which are accepted. Such norms are not static. They, being the crux of society, keep changing with the time, place and situation. In the context of change in the norms with the change of time and place, it has been said:

स एव धर्मः सोऽधर्मो देशकाले प्रतिष्ठितः ।

(Sa eva dharmaḥ sódharmó deśkāle pratiṣthitaḥ)

— *Mahabharata Shanti Parva (36-11)*

Fair conduct becomes misconduct with the change of place and time.

For example, addressing an elderly person as '*tu*' (तू) is a symbol of affection and nearness in western Uttar Pradesh, while it is taken as abusive and impolite in eastern regions. In olden days, son living separately from the parents was considered disrespect to parents, but these days parents do not mind such action. Same is the position of conduct in organisations in reference to discipline.

What is a Fair Conduct

The relevant point to consider then is, what a fair conduct is. A simple formula is:

शास्त्र प्रधाना लोक वृत्तिः ।

Śāstra pradhānā lok vṛttiḥ)

— *Chanakya Sūtram (469)*

General behaviour should be as per the principles established by the śastras.

In ancient time the *śastras*, the books of laws, rules, principles, injunctions etc used to guide the conduct of citizens. Various *śastras* used to guide the conduct in different areas, for example, we have *Dharma Śastra*, *Nyaya Śastra*, *Niti Śastra*, *Tark Śastra*, and so on. These *śastras* were the authorities and people were bound by duty to conduct themselves as per the principles laid down by the relevant *śastras*. That used to be the measure of a fair conduct and a disciplined life.

The other formula is:

स्वामिनमेवानुवर्तते ।

(Svaminmevanu vartate)

— *Chanakya Sūtram (340)*

The employee should obey the employer (the master).

This formula may not be taken in its face value alone. Never was the employee expected to obey the employer in a mechanical way like a slave. It was expected of an employee to abide by the norms established by the employer. The same practice continues even these days. The employers frame their rules and regulations and the employees are expected to act in accordance with them. That was and still continues to be a fair and disciplined conduct.

Self-Discipline

A disciplined way of life is simple to lead. Simply act as per the norms established by *śastras*, according to the way shown by the elders and be within the ambit of a disciplined way of life. If such becomes the way of life, that would be called self-discipline. Then nobody would be needed to supervise. Kautilya, in this context, has said:

विनयमूलो दण्डः प्राणभृतां योगक्षेमावहः ।

(Vinayamulo dandaḥ prānabhṛtāṁ yogkṣemā vahaḥ)

—*Artha Śastra (1-5-2)*

Administration of the rod (punishment), when rooted in self-discipline, brings security and welfare to the living beings.

This is the literal meaning of the word. The hidden meaning is that administration rooted in self-discipline or administration by a self-disciplined administrator alone can lead to prosperity and security of the people.

The statement shows beyond doubt that the administrator ought to be a self-disciplined person. It is only such person who can infuse discipline amongst the people, which can pave the way for prosperity and well-being of the organisation. Thus, according to Kautilya, self-discipline assumes supreme importance.

Training and Practice of Discipline

Constant training and practice of discipline is very important. Contributing to such ideas, Manu has said:

तेभ्योऽधिगच्छेद्विनयं विनीतात्मापि नित्यशः ।
विनीतात्मा हि नृपतिर्न विनश्यति कर्हिचित् ।।

(Tebhyoadhigacchedvinyaṁ vinitātmāpi nityaśaḥ
Vinitātmā hi nripatirna vinaśyati karhicit)

— *Manu Smriti (7-39)*

The administrator (King) living within the limits of discipline should every day acquire knowledge about discipline and the limits of it, from the teachers. The administrator (King) living within the ambit of discipline never decays.

Manu holds the views that:

- The highest authorities must listen to the counsel to learn the limits of disciplined life.
- The higher and the top management need constant training in the matters of discipline.
- It is the responsibility of the top level management to act strictly in a disciplined manner.
- Discipline percolates from the top to the bottom.
- A disciplined administrator ultimately succeeds and never faces downfall, as long as discipline is maintained.

Acquiring knowledge and practice of discipline and the limits of it has its own importance. The in-born traits of discipline are properly shaped only with the help of the acquired knowledge. The process of learning needs to be practised constantly and regularly. Thus, leading a disciplined life depends mostly on training. In this context of training, Kautilya has said:

कृया हि द्रव्यं विनयति ना द्रव्यम् ।
(Kṛyā hi dravyam vinyati nā dravyam)

— *Artha Śastra (1-5-4)*

Training disciplines suitable persons not the unsuited ones.

He further says:

विघानां तु यथास्वभावाचार्य प्रामाण्याद्विनयो नियमश्च ।
(Vidyānāṁ tu yathāsvabhāvācārya prāmānyādvinayo niyamaśca)

— *Artha Śastra (1-5-6)*

By accepting authoritativeness of the teachers in respective sciences, training and discipline, sciences can be acquired.

Kautilya was a teacher; he therefore possessed clear understanding about the efficacy of training and constant practice and learning of discipline. The two statements discussed here make it absolutely clear as to how important disciplinary training is. It appears that Kautilya was of the view that if such training is not taken on regular basis, the acquired knowledge loses its worth.

Further emphasising the need for training in disciplinary matters, it has been said:

विद्याविनीतो राजा हि प्रजानां विनये रतः ।
अनन्यां पृथ्वीं भुंक्ते सर्वभूतहिते रतः ।।
(Vidyāvinīto Rājā hi prajānāṁ vinye rataḥ
Ananyāṁ pṛthiviṁ bhunkte sarvabhuthite rataḥ)

— *Artha Śastra (1-5-17)*

The administrator (King), who is trained in the sciences aimed at disciplining of the people, enjoys the office (earth) for long, provided he is devoted to the welfare of all living beings.

Though Kautilya has said this in reference to the King enjoying his rule on the earth for long, but it equally applies to the administrators enjoying the office.

Multitude not to be Punished

The wise teacher could visualise many difficult situations. Sometimes, a stage comes when a large number of people indulge in misconduct, for example, participating in illegal strike and other such activities. In such a crisis, the Kautilyan prescription is:

दण्डो हि महाजने क्षेप्तुमशक्यः ।
(Dando hi mahājane kṣeptumśkyah)

— *Artha Śastra (9-6-3)*

Punishment cannot be used against a multitude of people. Alternatively, it may be said that disciplinary action cannot be initiated against a large number of people.

A practical view has been adopted in this statement. Initiation of disciplinary action against a large number may not be possible, as a whole department for such purpose may be needed. The more important reason is that it may not be fair to create an army of enemies to meet a crisis which could be resolved in other better ways. Some deft managers, in such situation, initiate action against some hardcore ones and some weaklings. The weak ones get scared, easily demoralised, which spreads and deters others. Leaving them in that situation, the counted few can be dealt with effectively. Of course, this is a cut-and-dried formula but only one of the several methods.

Scientific Base of Disciplinary Action

Disciplinary action has by now become very scientific and based on established norms. This is not a modern development, but has is its origin in the remote past. This would be clear thus:

> जानाति विश्वासयितुं मनुष्यान् विज्ञात दोषेसु दधाति दण्डम् ।
> जानाति मात्रां च तथा क्षमा च तां तादृशं श्रीर्जुषते समग्रा ।।
> (Jānāti viśāsyituṁ manuśyān vijñāt dośesu dadhāti dandam
> Jānāti mātrāṁ ca tathā kşmā ca taṁ tādŗśaṁ śrirjuşate samagrā)
> — *Mahabharata Udyog Parva (33-105)*
>
> *One who knows how to create confidence amongst people, who punishes only that person against whom charges have been proved, also knows the quantum of punishment to be given and also to pardon, that administrator gets all the advantages.*

The above quotation makes it clear that even during the Mahabharata period, such niceties of a disciplinary action were clearly known. Any administrator must know and understand the following procedure of punishment:

- Fair enquiry must be conducted.
- Punishment should be given only when the charges are proved.
- Punishment must be in proportion to the misconduct.
- Justice must be tempered with mercy.

Proportionality of Punishment

Each of the above points has been reiterated by the Supreme Court of India, time and again. Capacity to pardon, which has taken the shape of justice tempered with mercy, is a quality which touches the very theory of punishment — the corrective influence. The punishment which does not have a scope for correcting the delinquent is not a punishment in the right spirit. This spirit has been exhibited in various pronouncements of the High Courts as well as the Supreme Court.

The matter of proportionality of punishment, though the courts have recently started showing concern, but this remains an age-old concept. Chanakya has said:

अपराधानुरूपो दण्डः ।
(Aprādhānurupo dandaḥ)

— *Chanakya Sūtram (328)*

Punishment should commensurate the misconduct.

Consolidating the Chanakyan view, the *Mahabharata* says:

सम्यक प्रणयतो दण्ड।
(Samyak pranayto dandaḥ)

— *Mahabharata Shanti Parva (85-23)*

Punishment should be well-considered, just and reasonable.

The two injunctions convey, more or less, similar advice. While the earlier one emphasises only the proportionality of punishment, the later one gives some additional comments. A well-considered punishment must be based on fair enquiry, the intention and the repetitive character. Any just punishment is bound to be proportionate to the misconduct. A reasonable punishment shall be proportionate as well as containing the element of mercy.

Any punishment, in order to be effective and purposeful, must be well considered one. If it is not well-considered, how can it be just and reasonable?

What a well-considered conclusion is in the context of misconduct and punishment has been deliberated upon by 'Manu' as:

अनुबन्धं परिज्ञाय देश कालौ च तत्वतः ।
सारापराधौ चाल्केयं दण्डं दण्डयेषु पातयेत । ।
(Anubandhaṁ parijňāya deśkālau ca tatvataḥ

Sārparādhau cākleyam dandaṁ dandayeṣu pātyet)

— *Manu Smriti (8-126)*

The authority should punish the delinquent only after ascertaining the motive, the conspiracy, the time and place, physical and monetary capacities and the seriousness of the misconduct. Consideration of these concerns will tend to make the order of punishment judicious, thoughtful and fair.

The idea of proportionality of punishment has drawn the attention of the apex court only in the recent past. Such intervention was possible only after the inclusion of Section 11-A in the Industrial Disputes Act 1947, by Amending Act 45 of 1971. In one of the pronouncements, the Court observed, "In the development of industrial relations norms, we have moved from the days when quantum of punishment was considered a management function, with the courts having no power to substitute their own decision in place of that of the management. More often, the courts found that while the misconduct is proved, the punishment was disproportionately heavy. As the situation then stood, the courts remained powerless and had to be the passive sufferers, incapable of curing the injustice. Parliament stepped in and enacted Section 11-A of the Industrial Disputes Act 1947...."

This was all done so late in the day, whereas the scriptures had the foresight to prescribe that the punishment should be in proportion to the misconduct.

Element of Mercy

The concept of mercy demands consideration of the intention, whether the delinquent has committed the misconduct for the first time or he is a habitual one. The main point for consideration should be that the punishment has to be corrective and visible to others as well. This will also call for a prompt action. If it is found that the punishment to the delinquent may mean acute suffering to the innocent family members, the temper of mercy ought to be applied to the punishment.

Severe Punishment to be Counterproductive

It was well known to the ancient thinkers as to what could be the effect of harsh punishment. It has been said:

दण्ड पारुष्यात् सर्वजनद्वेष्यो भवति ।
(Danda parusyat sarvjana dveşo bhavati)

— *Chanakya Sūtram (76)*

One who inflicts harsh punishment earns enmity of all.

This formula indicates that punishment can be counterproductive. If, because of the harsh punishment, the subordinates are angry to the extent that they become the enemy of the boss, it is obvious that the production would suffer.

Mild Punishment Ineffective

As against the harsh punishment a mild one is also harmful. He says:

> तीक्ष्ण दण्डो हि भूतानामुद्वेजंनीयो भवति ।
> मृदु दण्डः परिभूयते यथार्हदण्डः पूज्यते । ।
> (Tekṣna dando hi bhūtānamudvejnīyo bhavati
> Mṛdu dandaḥ paribhūyate yathārhdandaḥ pūjyte)
>
> — *Artha Śastra (1-4-8, 9, 10)*
>
> *The administrator or ruler serving with the rod becomes a source of terror to his subordinates. The administrator mild with the rod is despised. The one just with the rod is honoured. Thus, the punishment must be just and well-considered.*

Fear of Punishment

However, the fear of punishment rather than the punishment has a magical effect. The formula is:

> न दण्डादकार्याणिं कुर्वन्ति ।
> (Na dandādkāryāni kurvanti)
>
> — *Chanakya Sūtram (82)*
>
> *For fear of punishment, people refrain from doing what they should not.*

Natural Justice

In the process of inflicting appropriate punishment, the rules of natural justice must be followed. This aspect too has not been missed by the ancient scholars. A lot has been said about freedom from bias, but other rules of natural justice have also drawn the attention of those scholars. Besides the presently established rules, something new has also been said in the context of natural justice. A famous rule is:

> आत्मनः प्रतिकूलानि परेषाम् न समाचरेत ।
> (Ātmanaḥ pratikulāni pareṣām na samācaret)
>
> — *Mahabharata*
>
> *Whatever is adverse to you, do not do the same to others.*

In the context of disciplinary action, the authority must place himself in the shoes of the charged person and judge for his own self if what he intends to do can be tolerated by his own self. This is the touchstone. If this rule is applied, the authority will not indulge in any wrong action. Though, this concept is not taken note of, yet, its utility can hardly be ignored.

Justice be seen to have been done

Then comes the other rule that 'justice should not only be done, but it should be seen to have been done'. This rule can be followed in many ways, one of which is that the person hearing a case should refrain from coming to a conclusion without hearing one party or the other. Śukra, while enumerating the five reasons for bias, names them thus:

> राग लोभ भयद्वेषां वादिनोश्च रहः श्रुति ।
> (Rāglobha bhaya dveṣā vādinośca raḥ śruti)
>
> — *Śukra Nitih*
>
> *Attachment, affiliation, fear, enmity and listening to either party in isolation or in private are the reasons for bias.*

The last reason is the deadliest of all. If the person responsible for dispensing justice possesses any one or more of the above said five reasons, his conduct will be opposed to the rules of natural justice. Supreme Court has pronounced many judgements in which, for the above reasons (one or more), the punishment has been set aside.

Not to Judge His Own Cause

The other rule of natural justice is that 'nobody shall be a judge in his own cause'. This rule is also covered by the aforesaid five reasons. If a person has his personal interest in a case, he will not be said to be the judge. The person who possesses attachment or affiliation with a case should not sit in judgement on that case.

Thus, Śukra's statement as aforesaid takes care of both the rules of natural justice, which must be followed by the person entrusted with the responsibility of dispensing justice.

Right to be Heard

The other principle of natural justice has been covered in the first two lines of the *śloka* quoted earlier from *Mahabharata* which say, 'the one who knows how to create confidence amongst people, who punishes only that person against whom charges have been proved'. The rule covered by these lines is, 'No one shall be condemned, unheard — the other side should also be heard'.

Only such person can dispense fair justice who allows fair hearing to both the parties. It is in such process that punishment shall be awarded only to that person against whom the charges have been proved. In the context of this rule of natural justice, one line of a *śloka* is:

नासम्पृष्टो व्युपयुंक्ते पदार्थे ।

(Nāsamprṛṣto vyupayunkte padārthe)

— *Mahabharata Udyog Parva (33-27)*

Do not say anything with regard to the one who has not been asked or questioned.

Wise persons do not frame opinion, draw conclusions or express views about any person without asking or questioning the other person concerned. This is the right to be heard — a rule of natural justice.

Freedom from Bias

The other aspect of natural justice is that the person dispensing justice should not have any bias against either party. The scripture says:

व्यवहारे पक्षपातो न कार्यः ।

(Vyavahāre pakṣpāto na kāryāḥ)

— *Chanakya Sūtram (546)*

There should be no favours or disfavours in the matter of dispensing justice.

Avoidance of such partial attitude should always be practised, not only in the matter of deliverance of justice, but also in administrative justice.

Sometimes, a bonafide act may appear to be a biased one. For preventing such wrong perceptions, the rule that 'justice may not only be done but should be seen to have been done' ought to be adopted. The administrative actions must be open to the public gaze to a reasonable extent. For example, the rules of promotion must strictly be followed in letter and spirit in such a way that the concerned person should be able to perceive that the same have been followed.

The five reasons for bias have already been discussed earlier under the sub-heading 'Natural Justice'. These five reasons have such wide scope that any other reason may be difficult to name. They also cover most of the rules of natural justice within their scope.

There are great possibilities of bias, if the dispenser of justice or the administrator hears or talks to either of the parties in private. To avoid such bias, Śukra issued two injunctions:

नेकः पश्येच्च कार्याणि वादिनो श्रृणुयादवचः ।
रहसि च नृपः प्रासः सभ्याश्चैव कदाचन ।।
(Nekaḥ paśycaca kāryāni vādino śnuyādvacah
Rahasi ca nṛpaḥ prājñah sabhyāscaina kadācana)

— *Śukra Nitih (4-5-6)*

The wise person dispensing justice should not examine the suits, or listen to the parties in private.

अति प्रत्यर्थि प्रत्यक्षं साधनानि प्रदर्शयेत ।
अपृत्यक्षं तयोर्नैव गृहणीयात साधनं नृपः ।।
(Ati pratyārthi prayakṣam sādhnaṁ pradaiśyet
Apratyakṣam tayornaiva gṛhniyat sādhanaṁ nripat)

— *Śukra Nitih (4-5-165)*

The person dispensing justice should examine the evidences in the presence of both the parties and not see the evidences or witnesses of either party in private, when the other party is not present.

Both these injunctions also form part of the rules of natural justice. All such administrators who perform any judicial or quasi-judicial functions ought to act accordingly; the reason being that the persons dispensing justice ought to have some special qualities.

Vedic Views

The qualities of the person delivering justice have been described in the *Yajur Veda* thus:

श्रुधिश्रुत्कर्ण वहिनिभिः देवै रग्ने सयावभिः ।
आ सीदन्तु बर्हिषि मित्रोऽअर्य्यमा प्रातर्यावाणोऽध्वरम् ।।
(Śrudhiśrukarna vahinibhiḥ devai ragne sayāvabhih
Ā sidantu barhiṣi mitro aryymā prātaryāvānaudhvaram)

— *Yajur Veda (33-15)*

The administrator keen to hear the applicant should be bright and powerful as fire. He should be learned, should come and sit to deliver justice along with the judicial officers having the qualities of deciding the case without violence, free from bias; they should be a friend of all, respectful for all and maintaining the dignity of all.

The unbiased character of the persons performing judicial or quasi-judicial functions had been in practice even in the Vedic period and so was the rule of natural justice — 'hear the other side also'.

Manu's Views

Manu has also issued injunction about the manner in which the cases should be decided. Here also bias has been forbidden. Manu has said:

एषु स्थानेषु भूयिष्ठं विवादं चरतां नृणाम् ।
धर्मं शाश्वतमाश्रित्य कुर्यात्कार्य विनिर्णयम् । ।

(Eşu stāneşu bhuyişthaṁ vivādaṁ cartaṁ nŗnām
Dharma śāśvatmāsritya kuryātkārya vinirnayam)

— *Manu Smriti (8-8)*

The cases should be decided on the basis of the perpetual duties (Dharma). There should be no bias.

Deciding the cases without bias should be the duty of the judicial, semi-judicial and administrative officers.

Equality before Law

No discussion on freedom from bias would be complete unless equality before law has been talked about. Most of the thinkers and scholars of the ancient period have propagated and issued injunction on the principles of equality before law. For example, Manu has said:

पिताचार्यः सुदृन्माता भार्या पुत्र पुरोहितः ।
ना दण्डो नाम राज्ञोस्ति यः स्वधर्मे न तिष्ठति । ।

(Pita acaryah sudrinmata bharya putro purohitah
Na dando nam rajnoasti yahsvadharme na tisthati)

— *Manu Smriti (8-355)*

If even the father, mother, wife, son, friend or teacher (guru) fail to follow their Dharma, they shall be liable to be punished.

The word *Dharma* used in these lines stands for the duties cast upon each for the welfare of the society, for example, *Sevaka Dharma*, *Pitri Dharma*, *Matri Dharma*, *Chhatra Dharma*, *Putra Dharma* and so on. If any one, may be the father, mother, brother, wife, friend or teacher, deviates from his duty, he shall be liable to be dealt with according to the law and face the consequences as any other citizen would. No one, howsoever close he may be to the corridors of power, can be given any preferential treatment before the law. Duties for everyone have been prescribed, which they are expected to follow.

As a support to this ancient order, the Constitution of India also has also provided for equality before law under Article 14. Such equality has been provided as a part of Fundamental Rights. This right is not subject to conditions. Under this provision, no one can be given any preferential treatment by virtue of his status. This, in other terms, can be called 'Rule of Law'.

Fundamental Duties

Ancient thinkers had prescribed the duties of various classes of people as *Dharma* but Indian Parliament by the 42nd Amendment in the Constitution in 1976, prescribed the Fundamental Duties for the citizens of India alone. While the right of equality before law is for all person (including even non-citizens), the duties prescribed are for the citizens alone.

Deliberating in the same context, Kautilya has said:

दण्डो हि केवले लोकं परम चेमम् च रक्षति।
राज्ञा पुत्रे च शत्रौ च यथादोषं समं धृतः ।।
(Dando hi kevale lokaṁ param cemam ca raksati
Rājňā putre ca śatrau ca yathādoṣam samam dhritaḥ)

—*Artha Śastra (3-1-42)*

It is the law (here dand means law) alone that guards this world and the other, when it (law) is evenly meted out by the King to his son and his enemy, according to the offence. This means that there should be no discrimination of any sort before the law.

This great right of equality before law is not flawless. When all are treated equal in the matter of application of rules (which too have the force of law), the star performer as well as the work shirker are to be treated as equals. In the process, the star performer is the sufferer. However, in spite of such odds, the equality cannot be compromised. As a way out, the management with foresight ought to take special care of such contingencies by suitably amending the rules.

Conclusion

If this principle of equality can be applied in awarding punishments too, there shall be hardly any ground for any grudge. However, discretion is necessary. Yet, Manu has prescribed lighter punishment to low-placed person as compared to high-placed ones. He pleads that the punishment should commensurate the social status, learning and prestige of the delinquents (see *Manu Smriti* — 8-337, 338). However, this is only a shade of opinion, which may lead to a number of confusions and complications.

The discussions so far show that Indian scriptures are full of highly developed principles in the whole field of discipline. They are the forerunners of the thought, theories and practices, which are often labelled as modern.

OO

12

The Regulatory Provisions

Ancient Industrial System

The industrial system in ancient India existed in a matured stage. There were factories producing textiles, metallic items, arms and ammunitions, chariots, and various other articles. Dockyards manufactured ships, boats and allied goods. Agriculture was in a developed stage. Mints produced gold, silver, copper and alloy coins that were current and legal tenders. Mining operations were carried out; there existed a distinct class of miners. Regular trade and commerce was in vogue. There were established land and water trade routes. Trading was extended even to gems, gold, silver, ivory and other precious materials. There were experts of various branches of trade and commerce. Various manufacturing operations employed artisans, craftsmen and experts too.

Natural consequence of such a developed system of industry was that there existed a distinct class of serving people called employees or workers. Trade unions also existed. Developed management concepts, like motivation, boosting the morale, incentives, and many others were practised. Social security was a prime concern to the employers and the state.

Such state of industry, economy and the society bears the testimony of Kautilya's *Artha Śastra*, Śukra's *Śukra Nitih* and Manu's *Manu Smriti*. A study of these works bring to light a variety of provisions, regulating fixation, forms and categories of wages, hours of work, rest intervals, layoff, sickness leave, provident fund, gratuity, pension, etc. Such provisions, though centuries old, are so relevant even today that the modern ones appear to be their replica.

Setting up Factories

Kautilya has expressed the view that incentives and motivations need to be used as early as the time of establishing the factories. He has said:

क्षौमदुकूलक्रिमितानरांकवकार्पास सूत्रवान कर्मान्तांश्च ।
प्रयुंजनो गन्धमाल्यदानैरन्यैश्चौपग्राहिकेराराध्येत । ।
वस्त्रास्तरणप्रावरणविकल्पानुत्थापयेत ।
कंटककर्मान्तांश्च तज्जातकारु शिल्पिभिः कारयेत । ।

(Kṣaumdukūlkrimitānrānkavkārpās śūthravān karmāntānśca
Prayunjano gandhmālya dānaira nyaiś caupagrāhi kairārādhyet
Vastrāstrana prāvaran vikalpyānutthāpayet
Kantak karmāntānśca tajjátii kāru śilpibhiḥ kāryet)

—*Artha Śastra (2-23-8, 9, 10)*

When starting mills for weaving cloth from ksauma, dukula, silk yarn, hairs of ranku and deer, and cotton yarn, he (the sutradhyaksha — superintendent of yarn and textiles) should gratify the workers by gifts of perfumes and flowers and by other means of showing goodwill. He should bring about the productions of variety of cloth, bedsheets and coverings. He should start factories for armours by artisans and craftsmen expert in the line.

The above lines show that there used to be factories manufacturing textiles of different varieties, armours and other articles. It has been prescribed that adequate incentive and motivational schemes ought to exist so as to attract the workers, craftsmen and experts. The motivational schemes should be so foresighted that the workers, artisans and the experts could easily be drawn towards the mills. This was necessary for the reasons that the people would be induced to come out of the village economy where they perceive the industry to provide higher benefits not only by way of wages but also non-monetary rewards to boost up the morale.

Other allied functions of the state are prescribed thus:

आकरकर्मान्त द्रव्यहस्ति वनव्रज वाणिकपथप्रचारान् ।
वारिस्थल पथपण्यपत्तनानि च निवेशयेत । ।

(Akarkarmànt dravya hasti vanvraj vanikpathpracārān
vāristhal pathpanya pattanāni ca niveśyet)

—*Artha Śastra (2-1-19)*

The state (King) should set up work in mines, factories, forest produce, elephants and cattle herds and should establish land routes, water routes and ports for trade.

The word '*panya pattana*' usually means a market town, but in the present context it refers to a port, not an inland town. This suggests that market towns were mainly situated on riverbanks or the seacoasts. This gives the idea about the highly developed state of trade and commerce. The trade was not only limited to inland market but was extended to overseas as well. The lines also bear the evidence of the existence of mines and mining operations. Forest products, like timber, elephants and cattle were also trade items, besides the gems and precious metals. Existence of established water routes shows the extent of export trade. All the trade activities had the protection of the state.

In the face of such developed trade, commerce and industry, the protection of interest of the workers by the state was necessary. The state being alive to such responsibility regulated the matter of wages in many ways. This is highlighted by:

कृत्यानि पूर्वं परिसंख्याय सर्वाण्यायव्यये चानुरूपान च वृत्तिम्।
संगृहीण्यादनुरूपान् सहायान् सहायसाध्यानि हि दुष्कराणि।।
(Kṛtyāni pūrvaṁ parisankhyāy sarrāvanyayavyaye
cānurūpān ca vrittim
Sangṛhenyādnurūpān sahāyān sahāyā sādhyāni hi duśkrāni)

— *Mahabharata Udyog Parva (37-24)*

After deciding the work, the budget and setting the reasonably fair wages, the employer should recruit suitable workforce, because of the reason that even the most difficult works can be successfully done with the help of an appropriate workforce. Thus, fair wages are of utmost importance.

Wages as Per Capacity to Pay

About the quantum of wages, it has been provided that:

दुर्गजनपदशक्त्या भृत्यकर्म समुदयपादेन स्थापयेत कार्यसाधन।
सहेन वा भृत्य लाभेन शरीरमवेक्षेत ना धर्मार्थौ पीडयेत्।।
(Durgjan padaśaktyā bhritkarm samudayapāden sthāpayet kāryasādhan
Sahen vā bhritya lābhen srīrmvekşet nāi dharmārthau pīdyet)

— *Artha Śastra (5-3-1, 9)*

In accordance with the capacity of the city and the countryside, the wages of the workers shall be fixed at quarter of the revenue or at a rate that may enable the works to be carried out. Employer should pay due regard to the body and the income of workers earned as wages, so that no harm is caused to either the material advantage or the spiritual well-being of the workers.

The principles discussed here are the forerunners of the modern theory propounded by the Supreme Court of India, where 'capacity to pay' has been accepted as the basis for wage fixation. Kautilya's thought is more precise and practical; he has suggested a ratio between the revenue and expenditure on wages. The quantum of wages is close to the principles of economics as well as social justice when the wage is said to take care not only of the physical needs but also spiritual needs. These modern concepts were in vogue in India centuries back.

Minimum Wages

The other principle of wage fixation was:

अवश्यपोष्य वर्गस्य भरणं भृतिकादभवेत् ।
तथा भृतिस्तु संयोज्या यद्योग्या भृतकाय वै ।।

(Avaśyapoṣaya vargasya bharanaṁ bhritikādabhavet
Tathā britistu sanyojyā yadyogyā bhritikāya vai)

— *Śukra Nitih (2-402)*

Wages should be determined in such a way that the worker can feed and maintain his own self and his dependents. On the other hand, wages may be fixed in keeping with the workers worth usefulness.

In the above principle, the concept of minimum wages has been discussed. No employer was expected to pay less than the minimum wages, yet care was to be exercised to ensure that no worker is paid less than what his worth deserves. Minimum wage was at that level at which the worker could subsist his own self and his family and not more than that. However, the quantum of wage must be matching with the workers abilities to work and yield results. The aspect shows that though the minimum wage was to be paid, yet the worker's capacity to produce was also to be kept into consideration. Thus, the socio-economic justice was never overlooked.

Dependents Considered in Minimum Wages

The ancient thinkers never lost sight of the dependents of the workers. They also thought that wages should be both in cash and kind. Kautilya has said:

षण्डवाट गोपाल कदासकर्म करेभ्यो यथापुरुष।
परिवायं भक्तं कुर्यात सपादपणिकं च मासं दद्यात्।।
कर्मानुरूपं कारुभ्यो भक्तवेतनम्।।

(Şandvāt gopāl kadā sakarma karebhyo yathāpuruṣa parivāyaṁ
bhakataṁ kuryāt, sapādpanikaṁ ca māsaṁ dadyāt
Karmānurupaṁ kārubhyo bhakta vetanam)

— *Artha Śastra (2-24-28, 29)*

To watchmen in vegetable gardens and in fruit and flower enclosures, the cowherds and serfs and labourers should be supplied food in accordance with the numbers of dependents on them, and also be paid wages of one and a quarter pana (पण) per month. The artisans should be given food and wages in conformity with their work.

Thus an image of welfare state emerges in which the provisions exist for feeding not only the workers but also their dependents. In addition to the food, the worker also received wages as prescribed or in accordance with the quality of their work and ability.

This is the concept of fair wages, where the employer provides the food and some money is also paid as wages for meeting the other needs. Wages have been prescribed for the majority of workers but skilled ones were to be paid as per their skill. In this way, the skill gets its due weightage in wage fixation.

The theory of wage fixation in food and money has been reiterated by Kautilya (see *Artha Śastra* — 2-24-28, 29) by saying that different amounts of food and wages should be fixed for regular and casual employees according to their skill and work. The aspect of wage to be in proportion to the skill, designation and work has been reinforced by Manu (see *Manu Smriti* — 7-125) as well.

Wage Agreements

Another principle of wage fixation has been provided by Kautilya thus:

यथा संभाषितं वेतनं लभेत।
कर्मकालानुरूपं संभाषित वेतनः।।
(Yathā sambhāṣitaṁ vetanaṁ labhet
karmkālā nurupaṁ saṁbhāṣit vetanaḥ)

— *Artha Śastra (3-13-27)*

Workers shall receive wages as agreed upon. If they are not agreed upon, then they should be paid in conformity with work and time.

Wage fixation by mutual settlement was frequent in those ancient days. However, if no settlement existed, the wage was to be paid as per work, ability and time taken to complete the work. Introduction of a new factor of time is indicative of important phenomena of work study, job analysis and time study, which are considered to be basically modern methods, but existed way back in 300 B.C.

The system of wage fixation by agreement on the basis of work and time has further been elaborated in the *Artha Śastra* thus:

शंख वज्र मणि मुक्ता प्रवालहाराणां तज्जात पुरुषैः।
कारयेत कृत कर्म प्रमाण काल वेतन फलानिष्पत्तिभिः।।
(Śankha vajra manimuktā pravālhārānāṁ tajjāt puruṣaih
kāryet, krit karm pramān kāl vetana phalāniṣpattibhiḥ)

— *Artha Śastra (2-22-5)*

In the matter of examination of conch shells, diamonds, gems and necklaces of pearls and corals, the employer should make valuation through experts in the line making an agreement with them as to the amount of work, time allowed or available and wages.

This is an example of wage agreements in respect of the experts dealing with precious stones trade. The inspection about the quality of precious goods can only be done by the experts. Their wages are to be fixed only by agreement, keeping in view the two variables, namely the quantum of work and the time to be consumed in accomplishing the same. This is yet another example of the fact that work and time study and job analysis systems were in vogue in the Kautilyan age.

The thought about wages of artisans being as per agreement in textile mills based on the quantum of work and time has been dealt by Kautilya (see *Artha Śastra* — 2-23-7) in the context of the duties of the superintendent who should maintain close contact with the artisans. This provision takes care that when the supervisor maintains a close contact with the artisans, their interest is sure to be safeguarded.

Wages as per Ability and Quantum of Work

Wage fixation of artisans in consideration of the quantum and quality of work was the system persistent in the ancient period. Śukra has said:

दृष्टवा कार्याणि च गुणांछल्पिनां भृतिमावहेत् ।

(Driṣtvā kāryāni ca gunānchilpinām bhritimāvahet)

— *Śukra Nitih (4-5-35)*

Wages of artisans should be fixed on the basis of their quality and work. Here the quality and work include the quality, capabilities and the experience of the artisan. Work includes the skill, expertise, general health and work culture of the technicians and artisans. It is, therefore, evident that the system of wage fixation was not arbitrary, but based on reasonable scientific principles.

Manu has also prescribed the minimum wages and has also affirmed the theory of wages in both cash and kind. His view is:

पणों देयेऽषकृष्टस्य षडुत्कष्टस्य वेतनम् ।
षण्मासिकस्तथाच्छदो धान्यद्रोणस्तु मासिकः । ।

(Panó deyeavkṛtasaya ṣadutkṣtasya vetanam
Ṣadmāsikastathāçchādo dhānyadronastu māsikaḥ)

— *Manu Smriti (7-126)*

Lowest or minimum wage for the lowest categories of employees should be at least one pana (पण) and higher categories should be paid six panas per day. Besides, they should be given one dron (64 seers) of food grains per month and the clothes to wear and to sleep every six months.

Since Manu's period was more ancient as compared to Śukra and Kautilya, the wages in kind had been fixed at more liberal level; yet the fact remains that the system of payment of wages in cash and kind, starting with the Vedic period, travelled through Manu, Śukra, Kautilya and others till the modern age.

Wages as per the Quality of Product

Yet another theory of wage fixation has been provided by Kautilya:

श्लक्ष्णस्थूलमध्यनां च सूत्रस्य विदित्वा वेतनं कल्पयेत
बहवल्पतां च।
सूत्र प्रमाणं ज्ञात्वा तैलामता कोद्भर्त नैरेता अनुगृहणीयात।।
तिथिषु प्रतिमानदानैश्च कारयितव्याः सूत्र ह्रासे वेतन ह्रासो
द्रव्यसारात।।

(Ślakşan sthulmadhyańā ca sutrsya viditvā vetanaḿ
kalpyet bahvlptāḿ ca
Sutrapramanaḿ jňātvā tailàmata
kodvart naireta anugŗhniyat
Tithişu pratimāndānaiśca kārāyitvayāh
Sutra hrāse vetan hrāso dravasārāt)

— *Artha Śastra (2-23-3, 4, 5, 6)*

Wages should be fixed after ascertaining the fineness, coarseness or mediocre quality of yarn and the largeness or smallness of quantity. After finding out the amount of yarn, the superintendent should favour the workers with oil, myroblan (a fine variety of palm), and unguents (ointments). On festive days, the workers should be made to work by honouring and providing them gifts. In case of diminution in the quantity of yarn, there shall be diminution of wages according to the value of the yarn.

These lines show that the wages used to be directly linked with productivity of the workers. Not only the total production, but the quality of the produce was also important. The finer the yarn, the higher were the wages, and the same principle was applied to the quantity of the product. In case of reduction in quality or quantity of the product, the wages too used to go down. So the concept of productivity-linked wages is, in fact, an age-old thought and practice.

Another aspect that comes to light is the existence of various incentive schemes, if the production targets were exceeded. The dignity of workers was also properly taken care of. The dignity of those who worked on festive days was highly elevated. All these considerations take due care of the human side and boost up the morale considerably.

These practices are catching up now, but they were also prevalent in ancient Indian industrial scene.

Wages Classified

Then comes the consideration for the kinds of wages. Śukra provides:

न कुर्याद् भृतिलोपं तु तथा भृति विलम्बनम्।
अवश्य पोष्य भरणा भृतिर्मध्या प्रकीर्तिता।।
परिपोष्याभृतिः श्रेष्ठा समानाच्छादनर्थिका।
भेवेदेकस्य भरणं यया सा हीन संज्ञिका।।
(Na kuryād bhritilopaṁ tu tathā bhritivilambnam
Avaśya poṣyā bharanā bhritirmadhyā prakirtitā
Paripoṣyābhritiḥ śresthā samānācchādanrthikā
Bhevedekasya bharanaṁ yayā sā hīn sangyikā)

— *Śukra Nitih (4-5-35)*

There should be no fraudulence in the payment of wages, which must be disbursed in time. That wage, which is just sufficient for satisfying the bare needs, is termed as 'madhyama' (मद्यम) or tolerable. That which can meet all the needs of food, clothing and shelter etc. is said to be 'śrestha' (श्रेष्ठ). Wage, just enough for subsistence of one person, is called 'hīn' (हीन).

In modern days too, there are three kinds of wages, namely minimum, fair and living wages, as existed in the ancient period as *hīn*, *madhyama* and *śrestha* which stand for minimum, fair and good living wages respectively.

Less than Minimum — Harmful

It has been a settled view of the Supreme Court of India that the industry that cannot pay the minimum wages to its employees has no right to exist. Somewhat similar were the views of Śukra:

ये भृत्या हीन भृतिकाः शत्रुवस्ते स्वयंकृताः।
परस्य साधकास्ते तु छिद्रकोश प्रजाहराः।।
(Ye bhrityā hīn bhritikāḥ śtruvaste svamkritāḥ
Parasya sādhkāste tu chidrakoś prajāharāḥ)

— *Śukra Nitih (2-403)*

Those who get mean or minimum wages are like enemies created by the employer. They can side with the opponent and noting any loopholes in the employer's system can adversely affect the employer's financial position and may cause suffering to the citizens.

Thus, the payment of minimum wages was highly looked down in ancient period, as compared to the modern days.

Wages Classified Otherwise

Further, there was another classification of wages as:

कार्यमाना कालमाना कार्यकालमितिस्त्रिधा ।
भृतिरुक्ता तु तद्विज्ञैः सा देया भाषिता यथा ।।

(Kāryamānā kālmānā kāryakālmitistridhā
bhritiruktā tu tadvijňaiḥ sā deyā bhāśita yathā)

— *Śukra Nitih (2-395)*

Piece wage, time wage and combination of piece and time wage are the three types of wages. Each worker should be paid as per agreement, which means that the wages should be paid at the same rate as agreed upon.

Piece Wage

Giving examples of each class, Śukra has said:

अयं भारस्त्वया तत्र स्थाप्यस्त्वे तावतिं भृतिम् ।
दास्यामि कार्यमाना सा कीर्तिता तद्विदेशकैः ।।

(Ayaṁ bhārastvayā tatra sthāpyastve tāvatim bhritim
Dāsyāmi kāryamānā sā kīrtitā tadvideśkaiḥ)

— *Śukra Nitiḥ (2-396)*

You carry this weight to that place and this much amount shall be given to you; this is a piece wage.

Time Wage

वत्सरे वत्सरे वापि मासि मासि दिने दिने ।
एतवतीं भृतिं तेऽहं दास्यामिति च कालिका ।।

(Vatsre vatsare vāpi māsi māsi dine dine
Etavatiṁ bhritiṁ teahṁ dāsyāmiti ca kālikā)

— *Śukra Nitih (2-397)*

You will get this much amount as wages per year, per month, per day. This is called payment according to period — time wage.

Combination of Both

एतावता कार्यमिदं कालेनापि त्वयाकृतम् ।
भृति मेतावतीं दास्ये कार्यकालमिता च सा ।।

(Etāvtā kāryamidaṁ kālenāpi tvyākṛatam,
Bhṛti metavatiṁ dāsye kārya kālimitā ca sā)

— *Śukra Nitih (2-398)*

For doing this much work in this much time, you will get this much amount. This is called wages based on both period and quantum of work.

Thus the three different classifications of wages have been explained with the help of examples. The employers and employees, in ancient period, were free to adopt any particular system of wage payment.

Incentive in Piece Wage

In case of piece-rate system of payment of wages, there also existed a provision (see *Śukra Nitih* — 2-397) that if an employee executed the work expeditiously or in excess over and above the normal output, he should be paid an incentive bonus at the rate of one-eighth of his wages plus the due wages for that period.

Wage Payment

The matter of payment of wages was regulated for the employer and the employee both. The employer was under the obligation to pay the wages without any fraudulent behaviour and on time. The employee was under the obligation to work.

This obligation has been reiterated by Kautilya as:

वेतना दाने दश बन्धो दण्डः षटपणों वा ।
अपव्ययमाने द्वादश पणों दण्डः पंचबन्धो व ।।

(Vetanādāne daśbandho dandah satapano vā
Apavyayamāne dvādaś panodandaḥ pancabandho va)

— *Artha Śastra (3-13-33, 34)*

In case of non-payment of wages, the fine is one-tenth or six panas. In case of denial, the fine is twelve panas or one-fifth.

The present Payment of Wages Act 1936, which regulates fair and timely payment of wages of workers, makes similar provisions. The Act regulates the obligations of both, the employers and the employees.

One of the provisions of Payment of Wages Act is that if the worker does not work, he is not entitled for the wages for that period. However, the Industrial Disputes Act, 1948 provides that if the worker reports to the employer for work and the employer does not give him work, the employee can be 'laid off' and in that event, the worker shall be entitled for half the wages without work. Kautilya has also considered this situation. First, he has given the views of the other authorities and then showing his disagreement with them, he proceeds to express his own views thus:

उपस्थितम्कारयतः कृतमेव विघाद इत्याचार्याः ।
नेति कौटिल्यः ।।
कृतस्य वेतनं नाकृतस्यास्ति ।
स चेदल्पमपि कारयित्वा न कारयेत
कृतमेवास्य विघात् ।।

(Upasthitam kāraytaḥ kṛtmev vidyād ityācāryāh
Neti Kautilyaḥ
Kṛtasya vetanaṁ nākṛtasyāsti
Sa cedalpmapi kāryitvā na kāryet kṛtmevāsya vidyāt)

— *Artha Śastra (3-14-6, 7, 8, 9)*

If the employer does not give work when the worker has presented himself for the work, the work shall be considered as done say the teachers. "No" says Kautilya. Wage is for the work done not for what has not been done. If after allowing even a little work to be done, the employer does not allow it to be done further, his work shall be considered as done.

No Work No Wages

Here, Kautilya, after rejecting the views of other authorities, propounds the theory of 'No work no wages'. This theory may appear to be harsh but has a practical importance. In the present circumstances, if the employers supported by the government adopt such policy, the industrial strike may see its end. It may be only a transitory policy, but is very essential in the present context in which the workers resort to strikes and put the people to ransom and then force the employer to accept the demand. If by any chance, the demands are not accepted, then they press for the wages for the strike period, which is usually granted. This gives encouragement for further strikes.

Modernity of Kautilyan View

The other aspect of the opinion of Kautilya is that he suggested such measures as are available in the modern industrial laws. He has not only done so but has also gone a step further to meet such situation where the laws are silent. For example, the worker takes his salary and wastes it in gambling and drinking and the dependents are left to starve. In a similar context, it is provided:

मातरं पितरं भार्या यः संत्यज्य विवर्तते ।
निगडैर्बन्धयित्वा तं योजयेन्मार्ग संकृतौ ।।
तदभृत्यर्धं तु संदद्यात्तेभ्यो राजा प्रयत्नतः ।।
(Mātraṁ pitaraṁ bhāryā yaḥ santyajya vivartate
Nigdairbandhyitvā taṁ yogyenmārga sankṛtau
Tadbṛtyadhaṁ tu sanddyattebhyo Rājā prayatntaḥ)

— *Śukra Nitih (2-398)*

The worker who without taking care of the subsistence of the father, mother, wife, and other dependents, spends the wages the way he likes, he should be arrested and kept in handcuffs and he should be made to clean the roads and pathways. Half of his wages should be given to the dependents.

This is a practical way of dealing with such kind of situations. Our modern legislatures and administrators ought to take guidance from such age-old provisions.

Obligations of Employees

Considering the obligations of the employees, the very obligation of the employees is twofold; firstly that the work should be done and secondly, the work must be of the desired standard and within the given time limits.

A worker who does work, when he is in receipt of the wages be dealt thus:

गृहीत्वा वेतनं कर्माकुर्वतो भृतकस्य द्वादश।
पणो दण्डः संरोधश्चा कारणात।।

(Grhītvā vetanań karmākurvato britkasya dvādaś
pano dandaḥ sanrodhaścā kārnāt)

— Artha Śastra (3-14-1)

Worker not doing the work after receiving the wages shall be fined twelve panas and detention till the work is done.

Fines constitute one of the legal deductions under the Payment of Wages Act. The source is:

भृतो नार्तोनं कुर्याधो दर्पात्कर्म यथोदितम्।
स दण्डय कृष्णलान्यष्टौ न देयं चास्य वेतनम्।

(Bhṛto nārton kuryādyo darpātkarma ythoditam
sa dańdya krishnlānyaṣtau na deyamcāsya vetanam)

— Manu Smriti (8-215)

The employee who does not do the work on his own will without being ill is entitled to fine of eight krinals and his wages should also not be paid.

This is a negative force that compels the workers to work honestly. There are yet other kinds of fines that can be imposed on the workers if found guilty of any misconduct. In this matter, Kautilya has provided (see *Artha Śastra* — 2-23-16) that there shall be a fine for workers in accordance with their offence. The provisions regarding fines in the Payment of Wages Act also impose such limits.

Dealing with such situation in which the time is exceeded or the work is not done as per the desired standard, it has been provided:

कालातिपातेन पादहीनं वेतनं तद्द्विगुणश्च दण्डः।
कार्यस्यान्यथाकरणे वेतननाशस्तद्द्विगुणश्च दण्डः।।

(Kālātipaten pādhīnań vetanań tad dvigunasca dandaḥ
Kāryasyānyathākarne vetannāśastddvigunaśca dandaḥ)

— Artha Śastra (4-1-5, 7)

If the worker exceeds the time limit for the work to be done, there shall be reduction in wages by one quarter and double that shall be the fine. For carrying out the work otherwise than as ordered, there shall be a loss of wages and double that as fine.

These are the obligations of the employees that the work be done within the stipulated time and be as per specifications.

Kautilya also prescribes (see *Artha Śastra* — 4-1-4) that the artisans should do the work at a proper place and in the prescribed time which should be made known to them. If there is no stipulation in that behalf, the work as per its nature can be done at other place as well. The example of this kind of work can be seen in *bidi* rolling, tailoring, embroidering and a host of other works.

Appreciation of Human Resource

Indian thinkers were aware that while other resources depreciate, it is the human resource that appreciates with the passage of time. The evidence can be seen as:

यथा यथा तु गुणवान्भृतकस्तदभृतिस्तथा ।
संयोज्या तु प्रयत्नेन नृपेणात्महिताय वै । ।
(Yathā yathā tu gunvānbhṛtkastadbhṛtistathā
Sanyojyā tu proyanena nŕipenātmahitāya vai)

— *Śukra Nitih (2-401)*

As the merit and usefulness of the worker increases, his wages should be increased. He should be paid according to his merits.

This is the forerunner of the modern system of annual increments and increase in daily wages as the worker becomes experienced.

Rest Intervals

No worker can be expected to work for long hours without some rest in between. In this matter, it has been provided that:

भृत्यानां गृहकृत्यार्थं दिवा यामं समुत्सृजेत् ।
निशि यामंत्रयं नित्यं दिनभृत्येऽर्धयामकम् । ।
(Bhṛtyānāṁ gṛhkṛtyārthaṁdiva yāmaṁ samutsṛjet
Nishi yāmtrayam nityaṁ dinbhṛtyetdharyāmkam)

— *Śukra Nitih (2-407)*

Workers should be allowed some time off during the day to attend to their domestic chores (work); this may be one prahar (3 hours) in the day and three prahars in the night. If he is only a day worker, he could be given only half a prahar off during the daytime.

Such hours of work indicate that for those who had to work round the clock, the total working hours were only twelve and for the day workers, only ten and a half hours. This was the situation much before Kautilya, that is, in 300 B.C. If these Indian standards are compared with the standards prevailing during the advent of British rule, when the working hours used to be from sunrise to the night hours, it can be appreciated how liberal the Indians were, which is indicative of our glorious past.

Sickness Leave

Being considerate enough for the contingencies like sickness of the employee, Manu provided:

> *आर्तस्तुकुर्यात्स्वस्थः सन्यथा भाषितमादितः ।*
> *सदीघस्यापि कालस्य तल्लभतैव वेतनम् ।।*
> (Ártastukuryatsvasthḥ sanyathabhaṣit maditaḥ
> Sadirghsyapi kalsya tallabhtaiv vetnam)
>
> — *Manu Smriti (8-216)*
>
> *If an employee, free from diseases, keeps on working as directed, ever falls ill, he should be given leave with wages for a long period.*

This social security measure is in vogue even today but with the difference that all employees are equally entitled for such leave irrespective of the fact whether he maintains good or bad health

Other Social Security Measures

There were many other social security measures that have been provided by the ancient thinkers. The one connected with wages is:

> *षष्ठांश वा चतुर्थांशं भृतेर्भृत्यस्य पालयेत ।*
> *दद्यात्तदर्धं भृत्याय द्वित्रिवर्षोखिलं तु वा ।।*
> (Şaşthānś vā caturthāńś bhŗterbŗtysya pålyet
> Dadyāttardhḿ bŗtyāya dvitrivarşakhlaḿ tu vā)
>
> — *Śukra Nitih (2-417)*
>
> *One-sixth or one-fourth of workers' wages should be retained as deposit and should be returned partly or fully as considered appropriate every two or three years.*

This provision is in a way a scheme of the Provident Fund or a Savings Scheme. If the period of return of the savings is extended till the end of service, it becomes Provident Fund. If not then it remains limited to a Savings Schemes only.

Social security schemes further provide for gratuity, pension and family pension thus:

सेवां विना नृपः पक्षं दद्याद भृत्याय वत्सरे।
चत्वारिंशत्समा नीताः सेवया ये न वै नृपः ।।
ततः सेवा विना तस्मै भृत्यर्धं कल्पयेत्सदा।
यावज्जीवं तु तत्पुत्रेऽक्षमे बाले तदधकम्।।
भार्यायां वा सुशीलायां कन्यया वा स्वश्रेयसे।
अष्टमांशं पारितोष्यं दद्याद भृत्याय वत्सरे।।
(Sevāṁ vinā nṛpaḥ pakṣam dadyād bhṛtyāy vatsare
Catvārinśtsamā nītāḥ sevayā ye na vai nripah
Tatah sevā vinā tasmai bṛtyadham kalpyetsadā
Yāvjjivaṁ tu tatputreakṣme bale tadadhakam
Bhāryāyām vā suśilāyām kanyayā vā svaśreyase
Aśtamānśam pāritośyaṁ dadyād bhṛtyāy vatsare)

— *Śukra Nitih*

After completion of forty years of service under the same employer, the employer (King) should pay to the worker half month's wages as a reward or presentation pay at the rate of each year of service — half month pay per year of service.

After completion of forty years of service, the employer (King) shall pay half the salary as pension during the lifetime of the employee. On his death, minor son be paid one-fourth of the wages. If there is no son, such employee's wife or daughter should be paid one-eighth of the wages for maintenance.

The gratuity, pension and the family pension scheme as provided by the sage are on a more liberal side as compared to the modern scheme. Quantum of pension was raised to half the salary from one-third as a result of the Fourth Pay Commission. However, the scripture provides for half the salary in such ancient a period. Deliberating further, in respect of the social security schemes, Śukra has said:

स्वामिकार्ये विनष्टो यस्तत्पुत्रे तदभृतिं वहेत।
यावद्बालोऽन्यथा पुत्र गुणान्दृष्ट्वा भृतिं वहेत।।
(Svamikārye vinasto yastataputre tad bhṛtim vahet
Yāvadvāloanyathā putra gunāndṛṣtvā bhṛitim vahet)

— *Śukra Nitih (2-416)*

If the worker dies on duty in exercise of his employer's task, his son should be paid his wages. After the son comes of age, attains majority, he should be placed in employment and paid wages according to his capacity and merits.

Making similar provisions, Kautilya has said:

कर्मसु मृतानां पुत्र दारा भक्त वेतनम् लभेरन्।
बालवृद्ध व्याधिताश्चैषा मनुग्राहयाः।।
प्रेतव्याधित सूतिकाकृत्येषु चैषामर्थमानकर्म कुर्यात्।।
(Karmsu mṛtānāṁ putra dārā bhakta vetanam labheran
Bālvṛdha vyādhitāścaiṣā manugrāhyāh
Pret vyādhit sutikā kṛtyeṣu caiṣāmarthmānkarm kuryāt)

— *Artha Śastra (5-3-28, 29, 30)*

Of those dying on duty, the son and wife will receive food and wages. Their minor children, old and sick persons should be helped. The employer should grant money and do honour on the occasions of death, illness and birth ceremonials.

It was employers' obligation that the dependents of the employee who died during the employment must be provided adequate security for subsistence. In the present industrial scene, such protection as employment of the ward of the deceased employee has appeared on the scene only a couple of decades back. Prior to that, the only protection available was compensation under The Workmen's Compensation Act, 1923.

Other Miscellaneous Obligations

The employer was also under the obligation to take care of the grievances of the employees. It has been said;

सुदर्शना हि राजन प्रजा रंजयन्ति।
(Sudarśnā hi rājan prajā ranjyanti)

— *Chanakya Sūtram (558)*

The employer (King) should regularly listen to the difficulties and problems of employees and keep them satisfied. General meaning of 'sudarśna' is one who looks pleased and handsome. Here, it means the person who has insight and bears a pleasant outlook.

The employer ought to possess insight into the grievances and problems of his workforce and also keep them happy with pleasant expressions. Such policy of regular redressal of grievances of the employees has many advantages. The employee free from grievance puts his whole into his work, is more disciplined and productive. He sets the tune of the organisation towards work culture. If the grievances are resolved in time, no big dispute can crop up.

Another obligation of the employer is to motivate the work force and keep their morale high. It has been said:

यथा गुणान्स्व भृर्याश्च प्रजा संरंजयेन्नृपः ।
शाखा प्रदानतः कांश्चिदपराम् फलदानतः ।।
अन्यान् सुचक्षुषा हास्यैस्तथा कोमलया गिरा ।।
(Ythāgunānsva bhŗyarśca prajā sanrańjyennŗpaḥ
Sākhā pradāntah kānścidparām phaldāntaḥ
Anyān sucayňuşā hāsyaisatathā komalyā girā)

— *Śukra Nitih (2-421)*

The employer (King) should preserve the virtues of the employees, make appropriate ordinary or higher rewards and keep them encouraged with sweet looks and soft words and thus serve the people.

This method, if adopted by the employers will elevate the morale of the people and motivate them to be a devoted and committed workforce. There is a lot of emphasis on the behavioural aspect of the employers in the scriptures.

Additional Wisdom

One of the managerial wisdom from *Mahabharata* says that only one person should be given a piece of work, not two or three. This is so for the reason that more than one person on the same job is not able to tolerate each other and there are usually differences in the opinions. This needs to be appreciated with sufficient clarity of thought. This will not apply where a team is allotted a job to perform. In case of the team, the situation is otherwise. There is no scope for difference of opinions in a team. The team members go with perfect understanding and this provision does not apply to a work team.

Trade Union

Trade unions existed mainly to protect the interest of working classes. Of late, a trend has set in, where a union has taken over the management of a factory, which being a sick unit was closed. It is possible that more such examples may come up in future; such efforts of trade union may be termed as teamwork. In ancient India, there used to be a distinct class of working called '*Sangh bhṛtāḥ*' (संघभृताः) or union workers. For them, Kautilya provides:

> संघभृताः संभूयसमुत्थारो वा यथा संभाषितं
> वेतनम् समं वा विभजेरन् ।
> (Sangh bhṛtāḥ sambhuya samutthāro vā yathā
> sambhaśitam vetanam samaḿ vā vibhajeran)
>
> —*Artha Śastra (3-14-18)*

Workers forming unions or partners in an undertaking shall divide the wages as agreed upon or in equal proportion.

Labour unions were a sort of partnership. Monetary transactions were rendered easy because of such unions. The labour unions had various kinds of workers, artisans, technicians etc. They used to undertake the work from the employers. This was a democratic method. The unions after finding out the labour's needs of the employers, used to discuss and settle amongst themselves as the union. Wages of different categories were mutually agreed upon. After finalising the deal with the employer, the union used to give a list of workers to them. Thereafter, the union was not free to change the workers without the consent of the employer. The worker was also not free to leave the union at that stage.

This system of labour union was in reality a partnership concept. When and why this system decayed is not known, but the present trade union system is a mutilated version of the old. If the ancient system gets revived, the industry is bound to take strides towards progress. The concept of employer as wage giver and labour as his own work seller are bound to disappear. The workers become their own employees or self-employed.

Industrial Disputes and their Adjudication

Disputes should be settled only on the testimony of witnesses. In the absence of witnesses, the judge should enquire at the place where the work was carried out.

Kautilyan sagacity may be witnessed that he could foresee the possible disputes in the matter of engagement of workers and also the system of wage payment. The simple way of settlement of such disputes was with the help of witnesses. But he could imagine that in some cases, there may not be a witness. In such events, he made the provision for judges who could settle the dispute. Such judges were not to depend on witnesses because the judge came into picture only in the absence of evidence of witness. The judge, so deciding the issue, was bound by the obligation to visit the work site to collect material that could help decision of the dispute.

The above system of settlement of dispute is the forerunner of the modern method of industrial adjudication now available in The Industrial Disputes Act, 1948.

Thoughts on Industrial Relations

One great factor that Kautilya has discussed, giving his own views and those of other sages, is practical and effective in the overall success of industrial undertakings. That is:

> क्षिप्रमल्पो लाभश्चिरान्महानीति वा क्षिप्रमल्पो ।
> लाभः कार्य दे कालसंवादकः श्रेयान इत्याचार्याः ।।
> नेति कौटिल्यः ।
> चिरादवि निपाति बीजसधर्मा महालाभः ।
> श्रेयान विपर्यये पूर्वः ।।
> (Kşipramalpo lābhaściran mahānīti vā kşipramalpo lābhah
> karya de kal samvādakaḥ śreyān ityāchāryāh
> Neti kautilyaḥ
> Cirādavi nipāti bījsadharmā mahālabhaḥ
> śreyān viparyaye pūrvaḥ)
>
> — *Artha Śastra (7-9-50, 51, 52)*
>
> *As between a small but quick gain and a large gain after a long time, the small but quick gain is preferable, if in consonance with the undertaking, the place and the time, so say the*

teachers. 'No' says Kautilya. A large gain after a long time is preferable, if not liable to disappear and if in the nature of a seed, in the reverse case the former.

Small and Quick Gain

Usually people are tempted by small and quick gains. In the industrial relations scene, general tendency is to find an ad-hoc solution. In this temptation, the managements many a times adopt policy of appeasement. Taking an example, the employees of a local body resorted to strike for some of their unrealistic demands. This lasted for about forty days. The workers and their leaders realised that the demands could not be met. Then they started negotiating for pay for the strike period. The authorities accepted the lesser evil and agreed. The roads in the town were jammed with heaps of garbage, which took another week to clear. Infections of various kinds had gripped the citizens who were left to their fate and the striking workers got their wages in full. Was such small and quick gain any good in the social interest? 'Kautilyan' policy does not approve such approach.

Large Gain after a Long Time

In another example again, the employees of a local body went on a strike in support of some unreasonable demands. The strike was so timed that it started some fifteen days before Deepavali when almost all the houses are cleaned. There was heaps of garbage on the roads. The administration had made it very clear that the demands could not be accepted. The unions and workers felt that a day or two before the festival, the administration would be compelled to agree. However, the administration made it clear that they were firm on their decision seeing that the union were adamant and were becoming unreasonable as they were putting the citizens to ransom. A solution was explored, under the supervision and security of the jail authorities, the prisoners were assigned the task of disposal of all the garbage and cleaning the city, a day before the festival. In return, the convicts were allowed remission of one to two months and also the regular wages. The convicts completed the work in record time and the citizens found the city cleaner that year as compared to the previous ones. The striking unions were demoralised and frustrated and wanted to negotiate on pay for the strike period. But the authorities were firm and did not agree. However, the strike was called off unconditionally. Thereafter, that city never faced a similar situation. Now, this acted as a seed for future. This is what Kautilya emphasises that a large gain after a long time is preferable, if the result is not likely to disappear and is in the nature of a seed.

Another allied wisdom from Kautilyan writing deals with the gains. He says:

> समे हि लाभे संधि स्याद्विषमे विक्रमो मतः ।
> समहीन विशिष्टानामित्युक्ताः संधि विक्रमाः ।।
> (Same hi lābhe sandhi syādviṣme vikrmo mataḥ
> samhin viśiṣṭānāmituktaḥ sandhi vikramāḥ)
>
> — *Artha Śastra (7-8-34)*
>
> *When the gain is equal, there should be peace; when unequal, war is considered desirable for the equals, weak and stronger.*

This writing is connected with peace and war between kingdoms, but contains practical consequences for the industrial scene as well. In the matters of collective bargaining, both parties weigh the benefits. But the fact remains that a blending of both interests is the interest of the undertaking. When both parties act wisely and keep the interests of both as equal, there is harmony that lasts long. But if one gains and the other does not and there is an agreement and truce as a result thereof, there is always a danger of strike. Therefore, this consideration ought to be borne in mind by all the concerned parties in the industry.

Conclusion

The foregoing points are not all that are available in Indian scriptures, which deal with much more. Yet, the relevant points have been highlighted in the hope that some day and from some others more and more would see the light of the day. The basic conclusion is that the modern thoughts in this area of management too are not new. Much developed thoughts existed in ancient India long back in the past.

OO

13

Training

Training of the personnel at all levels is gaining high importance in the modern management practice. However, this is only a revival of the idea, which had gone into oblivion. In ancient India, training was valued very high. Kautilya attached great emphasis to training, the obvious reason being that he was basically a teacher. He could visualise that the formal education provides information in the shape of knowledge, which when put to practice and tests transforms into experience.

Need for Training

Dealing with the need for training Kautilya has said:

> अविद्या विनयः पुरुष व्यसन हेतुः ।
> अविनीतो हि व्यसन दोषान्न पश्यति ।।
> (Avidyā vinayaḥ puruṣ vyasan hetuḥ
> Avinito hi vyasan doṣanna paśyati)
>
> — *Artha Śastra (8-3-1, 2)*

Absence of training in the learning of doctrines is the cause of man's vices. An untrained person devoid of learning is not able to visualise faults in the vices.

Learning of doctrines means not only collection of information but also sound and practical knowledge about them. The complete knowledge of doctrines comes through the process of training. A person, who does not acquire training of the doctrines, is not able to identify the vices, which keep on multiplying.

One can collect information from books, but the knowledge latent in a learned mind can be gained only by training.

An educated person remains only a raw material; he gets transformed into a resource only after acquiring knowledge about the secrets and niceties of the profession through the process of rigorous and continuous training. Training makes a man a thorough professional, but it should be a continuous process so that one is always updated about the latest and the emerging trends.

Source of Training

Emphasising the need of training, it has been said:

नित्यश्च विघा वृद्ध संयोगो विनय वृद्धयर्थम
तन्मूलत्वाद्विनयस्य।
(Nityaśca vidyà vṛddha sanyogo vinaya
Vriddhayartham tanmulatvàdvinayasya)

— *Artha Śastra (1-5-11)*

One should have constant association with elders in learning for the sake of their own training, since training has its deep roots in association with elders.

Training is largely based on learning. Elders have been recognised as the main source of training. They, in their own time had acquired knowledge, which had been tested to become experience. On the basis of such knowledge and experience, they are able to guide the younger generation so that they may become wiser. It is, therefore, necessary that those interested in acquiring training, so as to face and resolve various situations, should go to elders, who are competent enough to impart learning and training. It is from them that knowledge percolates and the persons in their association get trained.

Efficacy of Training

Commenting upon the efficacy of training, it has been said:

श्रुताद्धि प्रज्ञोपजायते प्रज्ञाया योगो।
योगादात्मवचेति विघानां सामर्थ्यम।।

(Śrutāddhi prajňopajāyate prajňāya yogo
Yogādātmavatteti vidyānaḿ sāmarthyam)

— *Artha Śastra (1-5-16)*

Continuous study awakens the intellect. From trained intellect, comes the practical application and from that comes self-possession of capabilities.

T. S. Eliot has said:

"Where is life we have lost in living;
Where is wisdom we have lost in knowledge?
Where is the knowledge we have lost in information?"

Process of Training

Simple reading or continuous study provides only information. The information thus collected has got to be converted into knowledge. The knowledge has then to be transformed into wisdom, as depicted in the given figure.

The knowledge brought into practice as a result of training gets transformed into wisdom, which we call 'trained intellect'. This trained intellect, on further training can be put to more practical application and makes oneself more capable. Such capability makes one competent enough to face the problems of life and self-confident. The process can be seen in the given figure.

A knowledgeable person, on receiving training, acquires higher or trained intellect — the art of applying knowledge. Such a person develops self-confidence and becomes capable of taking his own decisions. This is the stage when the person visualises the truth — the real understanding.

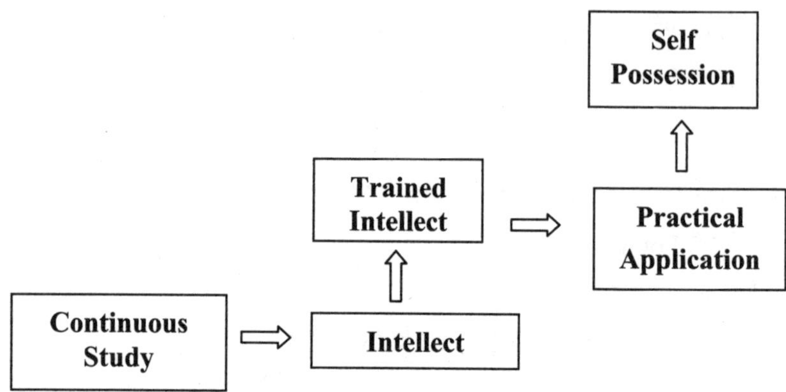

A young engineer fresh from the engineering college, possesses the information and knowledge about the Subject. Yet, he finds it difficult to apply his knowledge into practice unless he has undertaken practical training; so is the case with the manager who has to learn how to take decisions, which is an important attribute of managers.

A manager or administrator who has not received training is not well-equipped for the job. He, therefore, learns only by the 'trial and error' method. Therefore, the scientific approach is to provide suitable training as per the needs and suitability.

Qualities of a Trainee

Regular training is, therefore, very important in the matter of learning. Yet, the training programme in itself may not produce the desired results. The person, who receives training, is equally or in some way more important, as may be clear from the following observation of Kautilya:

शुश्रुषा श्रवण ग्रहण धारण विज्ञानोहापो।
हतत्त्वाभिनिविष्ट बुद्धिं विद्या विनयति नेतरम्।।
(Śśruṣā śravan grahan dhāran vijňānohāpo
hatattvābhiniviṣta buddhim vidyā vinayati netram)

— *Artha Śastra (1-5-5)*

Study of sciences imparts learning to one who has the desire to learn, listen and then to retain through understanding, rejection of false views and intentness on truth. He should not listen to any other person. This shows that everyone cannot improve from training. Only those, who possess the aforesaid qualities, can get results.

Desire to learn is the first pre-requisite. The one having desire to learn listens to the teacher attentively and learns in the process retaining what he has learnt. Then comes the understanding — proper appreciation of what has been learnt — its practical application. Then it is also necessary that the person learning ought to shed the false views that he might have taken. Finally, he has to fix his mind on truth alone as explained in the given figure.

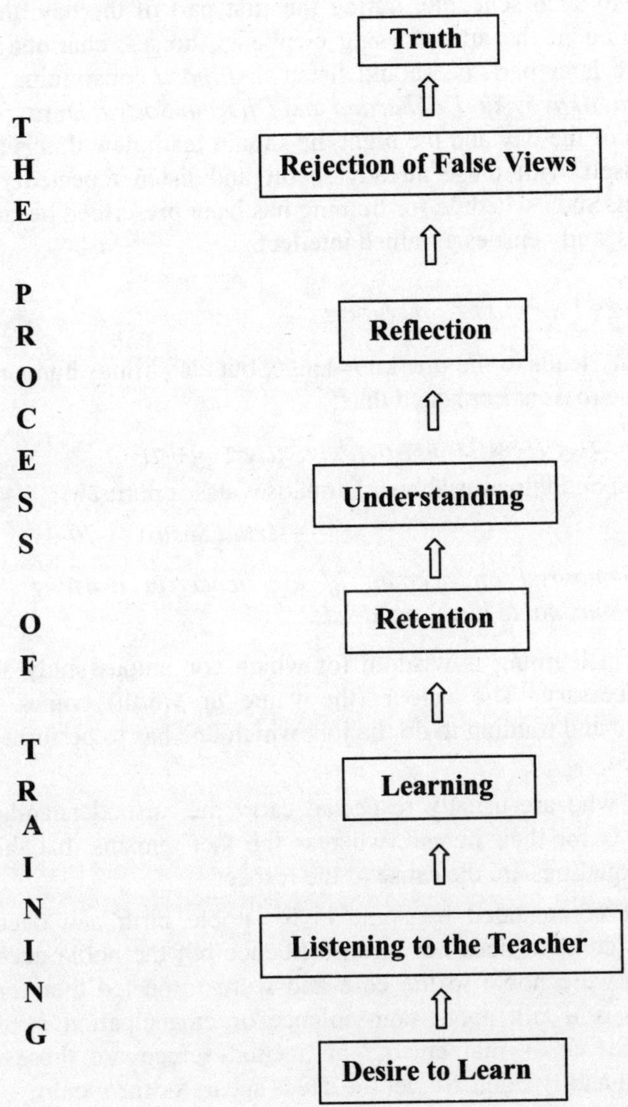

The desire to learn ultimately culminates in truth. The persons possessing such characteristics alone are qualified to receive training. It is on this basis that Kautilya has said that only suitable persons learn from training, not the unsuitable ones.

Kautilya has gone to the extent of prescribing the training schedule for princes, which can be taken as a guideline for training the executives (see *Arth Śastra* —1-5-12 to 15).

According to such schedule, during the first part of the day, there should be training in the arts of using elephants, horses, chariots and weapons. In the later part, he should listen to *Itihāsa* constituting the *Purānas*, *Itivrtta*, *Akhyāyikā*, *Udāharana* and *Dharma Śastra*. During the remaining parts of the day and the night, he should learn new things and familiarise himself with those already learnt and listen repeatedly to things not learnt. Such schedule for training has been prescribed because from continuous study ensues a trained intellect.

Training Brings Honour to Trainee

Training, not only leads to the true knowledge, but also brings honour to the person for the reasons explained thus:

पूज्या विद्या बुद्धिपौरुषाभिजनकर्मातिशयतश्च पुरुषाः ।
(Pūjyā vidyā buddhipauruṣābhijankarmātiśayataśca puruṣāḥ)

— *Artha Śastra (3-20-23)*

Men are honoured on account of excellence in learning, intellect, valour, noble birth and deeds.

Excellence in learning is wisdom for which continuous study and training are necessary. The valour (the value or worth) comes by learning, practice and training to do the job, which one has to perform or has been assigned.

The people who are usually respected carry the misunderstanding that the respect is for their person, whereas the fact remains that their capabilities and qualities are the cause of the respect.

The respect commanded by some is for noble birth and deeds. Nobility, in this context, does not mean affluence but the noble deeds. The great sages were noble to the core and were respected therefore. Whenever there is a talk about non-violence or emancipation of the downtrodden, the names that emerge on mental screen are those of Mahatma Gandhi and Buddha. So, let the deeds speak for the men!

Conclusion

The foregoing discussion shows that training till today is one of the most important management functions, as it has a direct bearing on human resource development. Training has the potential for leading towards excellence in man-management. Though other sages have also deliberated upon the training aspect but the Kautilyan approach is the most accomplished one as training falls within the proper scope of the function of teacher. If only the managements of the present organisations had properly appreciated the usefulness of training, the results would have been otherwise. However, it is never too late in the day.

○○

14

Money Management

Development of the Thought

The thoughts about 'money management' draw the attention of modern management experts in the advanced stage of development of management science. However, the concept has its roots deep into the past. The thoughts of Śukra are relevant even today as the modern ones are. Śukra has conceived and contributed original ideas about earning, spending, accounting, protection of money, public borrowing, lending, rates of interest and a host of incidental thoughts. These thoughts are like formulae that have borne the test of time and are as fresh as freshness could be.

"Material well-being is supreme," says Kautilya in *Artha Śastra* (1-7-6, 7). Developing the thought further, he says, "Physical and good sensual pleasures depend on material well-being." Money is the main source of material well-being. Therefore, the highest priority goes to money.

However, earning money, possession and accumulation thereof can hardly stand guarantee for the material well-being. The most important factor remains its proper management. Therefore, money management ought to be appreciated by the managers. The modern thoughts on money management, if supplemented by the ancient thoughts would be more beneficial and practical too.

Income and Expenditure

Defining the 'income' and the 'expenditure', Śukra has said:

वत्सरे वत्सरे वापि मासि मासि दिने दिने।
हिरण्यपशुधान्यादि स्वाधीनं त्वायसंज्ञकम्।।
पराधीनं कृतं यत्तु व्ययसंज्ञंधनं च तत्।।
(Vatsre vatsare vāpi māsi māsi dine dine
Hiranapaśudhānyādi svādhinaḿ tvāysanjaňakam
Parādhinaḿ kŗtain yattu vyayasaḿjnḿdhanaḿ ca tat)

— *Śukra Nitih*

The gold, cattle and food grains that get accumulated with a person is known as 'income', and the gold or other wealth that goes in the custody of others is called 'expenditure'.

These definitions indicate that Śukra had a clear vision that property did not mean only money. Other possessions, like cattle, food grains, land, gold and silver, were also regarded as wealth and their acquisition was included in income. The income may be of an individual, organisation, village or state, and could be daily, monthly or yearly. The expenditure was that part of the wealth that was given away to others for various considerations.

Śukra has further classified income and expenditure into different categories. For example, the income may be the current income or the accumulated one. Similarly, the expenditure too may be the consumed one or the one given in return of other commodities. Then, he has drawn finer distinctions of various categories.

The expenditure has been divided into three categories:

मूल्यत्वेन च यद्दत्तं प्रतिदानं स्मृतं हि तत्।
सेवाशौर्यादिसंतुष्टैदत्तं तत्पारितोषिकम्।।
भृतिरूपेण संदत्तं वेतनं तत् प्रकीर्तितम्।।
(Mulyatven ca yaddattaḿ pratidānam smritamhi tat
Sevāsauryādisantusataidattaḿ tatpāritoşikam
Bhritirupen saḿdattaḿ vetanaḿ tat prakirtitam)

— *Śukra Nitih (2-342, 343)*

The amount paid as the value is called '*pratidan*' or the price. Any amount or wealth paid in appreciation of service or bravery or some other good deed is called reward. The amount or commodities paid to the employees for their livelihood is called wages. These are simple definitions, but describing them is equally important in the context of money management so that the expenses incurred may be rationally classified. This becomes necessary as the thought goes up to departmental budget. It has been said:

यन्निमित्तो भवेदायो व्ययस्तन्नामपूर्वकः ।
व्ययश्चैव समुद्दिष्टौ व्याप्यव्यापक संयुतः ।।
(Yannimitto bhavedāyo vyayastannāmpurvakah
Vyayaścaiv samuddiṣto vyāpyavyāpaksaṁyutah)

— *Śukra Nitih (2-336)*

The income from a department is spent for the same. The right to spend vests with the same department, which earns the income. As the income depends upon the particular resources out of the total resources, so the expenditure is also incurred under some heads alone and not on all.

The income and expenses both are limited to some heads out of the numerous ones. This shows that proper accounting system based on the earnings and expenses of various departments existed and there was a clear understanding in such ancient a period.

Prevalence of Coins

The wealth, in the shape of gold, cattle and food grains was not the only form. There used to be gold, silver and copper coins also. The text goes:

रजतस्वर्णताम्रादि व्यवहारार्थ मुद्रितम् ।
व्यवगर्यवराटाद्यं रत्नान्तं द्रव्यमीरितम् ।।
सपशुधान्यवस्त्रादि तृणान्तं धनसंज्ञकम् ।।
(Rajata swarnatamradi vyavhararthmudritam
Vyavagaryamvaratādyam ratnānta dravamiritam
Sapasudhānya vastrādi trināntam dhanasangykam)

— *Śukra Nitih (2-356, 357)*

Coins made of gold, silver, copper and the shells shall be used by the people. All such coins shall be legal tenders. Besides, the precious stones, cattle, food grain, clothes and all other commodities shall be treated as wealth. The values fixed by the state (King) in terms of gold and other coins shall be recognised as the prices for such things.

The practices described in this couplet are relevant even today as they were in ancient times in India. The coins of different metals are minted and they are recognised as legal tender.

Spending Money

Earning and spending of wealth are equally important. The wisdom of proper utilisation of wealth has been dealt thus:

कृत्वा स्वान्ते तथौदार्यं कार्पण्यं विहिरेव च।
उचितं तु व्ययं काले नरः कुर्यान्न चान्यथा।।
(kṛtvā svānte tathaordāryṁ kārpanyam vihireva ca
Ucitaṁ tu vyayaṁ kāle naraḥ kuryānna cānyathā)

— *Śukra Nitih (3-195)*

One should spend reasonably with a generous heart but thriftily and timely. The couplet depicts four main features of proper use of money. Firstly that spending of money should be based on noble and bountiful nature. Secondly, while spending in a liberal manner, one must remain spendthrift. Such makeup of the personality takes to the third feature, that money must be spent reasonably and on appropriate juncture. Fourthly, that one should not indulge in spending otherwise.

There are people, who spend wealth only for the show of it and go to the extent of indulging in vulgar use of wealth. Many adorn the bridegroom or some special person with garlands made of currency notes. Some adorn a VIP with a gold crown. Such wastage of money is prohibited in the scriptures as the above example clearly shows.

Spending of money unwisely and not spending on the appropriate occasions has been further elucidated by Śukra thus:

बह्वर्थं न त्यजेदल्पहेतुनाऽल्पं न साधयेत्।
बह्वर्थव्ययतो धीमानभिमानेन वै क्वचित्।।
बह्वर्थव्ययमीत्या तु सत्कीर्तिं न त्यजेत् सदा।।
(Bahvarthaṁ na tyajedalpahetunālpam na sādhyet.
Bahvarthaṁ vyayato dhimānbhimānen vai kvacit
Bahvartha vyayabhityā tu satkīrtiṁ na tyajet sadā)

— *Śukra Nitih (3-227, 228)*

Wise people should not refuse to accept large sums of money for trifling assignments. They should also not spend heavy amounts for ordinary works only for the show of it; they should spend the money matching with the job. Also, they should not refrain from attaining higher distinction on the plea that the expenses shall be of a very high order.

The wisdom contained in the above lines is quite relevant to the modern days. In a self-styled ego, there are people who refuse to accept any money for trifling jobs or charge very little. Analysing this, it emerges out that if the job was really trifling why one would offer a high amount. On the other hand, not charging anything or undercharging adversely affects the importance of the job and the work is not cared for. Same way, the overspending for ordinary assignments shows that the person spending has lots of money and then people try to grab that one way or the other. The last advice is equally sagacious that when it comes to attaining distinctions, one must be prepared to spend fairly higher amount of money. Money should not be material in the matter of earning distinctions. The distinctions do not come alone; they are accompanied by lots of money and the future prospects become bright, which in itself has the potential for bringing more and more wealth.

Earning Spending Ratio

Deliberating on the ratio of earning and spending the wealth, it has been said:

यो जानात्यर्जितुं सम्यगर्जितं न हि रक्षितुम् ।
नातः परतरो मूर्खो वृथा तस्यार्जनश्रमः ।।

(Yo jānātyarjitum samyagarjitam na hi rakşitum
Nātaḥ partaro murkho vrithā tasārjanshramah)

— *Śukra Nitih (4-2-36)*

The one who knows how to earn but not how to protect wealth and put it to improper spending is an unwise person, as all his efforts of earning go waste.

Spending money conveys the idea of spending thoughtlessly or in an unplanned manner. However, reasonable spending may be said to be planned utilisation. The concepts of proper use and misuse also get attracted in analysis. While planned spending connotes useful expenditure, the extravagant spending tends to mean misuse. However, the expression may mean differently according to the person, situation, amount, region and time.

Śukra also says in *Śukra Nitih* (4-2-32) that the wealth acquired and accumulated must be protected because procuring and securing of wealth is a tedious job and its preservation is a fourfold process. Preservation of wealth includes safety as well as ensures its constant growth.

Wise Spending

Consolidating his view about prudent spending of wealth, Śukra has further said:

संरक्षयेत कृपणवत काले दद्याद्विरक्तवत् ।
मूर्खत्वमन्यथा यास्ति स्वधनव्ययतोऽपि च ।।

(Saurakşyet kripanvat kāle dadyādviraktvat
Mūrkhatvamanyathā yāsti svadhanavyayatopi ca)

— *Śukra Nitih (4-2-39)*

One should protect his wealth as a miser (kripan) does and spend it without any attachment when the appropriate occasion comes; otherwise he is caught in an unwise act of misuse of his well-earned money.

The word '*kripan*' or miser is used for such a person who prefers to live miserably only for hoarding money. He hoards wealth at all cost, not willing to spend any amount come what may. It is not Śukra's intent to use the word in that sense. This will be clear from the spending part in the same line. Here the word *kripan* has been intended to mean the one who protects his money against the misuse of wealth. In order to avoid wasteful use of money, one may at times protect it with all force. Yet, when the appropriate occasion comes, one should spend it generously. Precisely, one ought to be a spendthrift person.

Śukra uses the word '*murkha*' or a fool in the second line of the couplet. By *murkha*, he means an unwise, unenlightened and less prudent person. It is in this context that he says that a person who does not act sagaciously in protecting and spending the wealth is not wise, because he puts in all his precious efforts and hard work in earning and then puts it to wasteful purposes or indulges in extravagance.

Accounting Wealth

Commenting upon the accounting process, the scripture says:

नैवास्ति लिखितादन्यत् स्मारकं व्यवहारिणाम् ।
न लेख्येन विना कुर्याद् व्यवहारं सदा बुधः ।।

(Naivāstilikhitādanyat smārkaṁ vyavhārinām,

Na lekhyen vinā kuryād vyavahāraṁ sadā budhaḥ)

— *Śukra Nitih (3-189)*

There is no better way to keep monetary transactions in memory for a business person than to write them down. Therefore, a wise person should never enter into monetary transactions without writing them.

Perhaps, inspired by Śukra's thought, a maxim in Hindi came up as:

पहिले लिख पाछे को देय, भूल परे कागद से लेय।

(First write down and then give. In case of any discrepancy, take the money from the paper.)

Thus, the scripture lays down a practical yet simple method for accounting of wealth which is foolproof. This system of writing the money transactions forms a part of money accounting.

The Accountant

Managing the household transactions can easily be done by individuals. But for organisations, like shops, establishments, factories and a host of others, the work is assigned to professionals in the present management system. The same system has been conceived by Śukra. About the professional accountants, he says:

आवर्तकविहीनौ तु व्ययायौ लेखतो लिखेत्।
क्रयायधर्मण घटनान्यस्थलाप्तो विवर्तकः ।।
द्रव्यं लिखित्वा दद्यात्तु गृहीत्वा विलेखेत्स्वयम्।
हीयते वर्धते नैवमायव्ययविलेखकः ।।

(Āvartak vihīnau tu vyayāyau lekhato likhet
Krayādharman ghatnānyasthalāpto vivartakaḥ
Dravyam likhitvā dadyāttu grihitvā vilekhtasvayam
Hiyate vardhate naivamāyavayaya vilekhkaḥ)

— *Śukra Nitih (2-350, 351)*

The accountant should write down the expenses and the income which are likely to be ploughed back or not and all the monetary transactions. The accountant should himself write, give and accept the bills of income, expenditure, loans and borrowings etc. If the income and expenditure is written by the professional accountants, there is no excess or shortfall in the wealth.

The advanced stage of money management as conceived by the sages thousands of years back are still modern. The professional accounting system was developed much late in the management system. The professional charter of the ancient can be visualised by the designation '*Vyayayan Lekhtaḥ*' — the one who writes the expenses and the income. Those professional accountants were the experts who knew the intricacies of the trade. Their writing was accepted as authentic and the book written by them was honoured in the field of trade or business.

Interest Rate

Interest rates on borrowing and lending were also relevant in the ancient period. It has been said:

दृष्टवाऽधमर्णं वृद्धयापि व्यवहारक्षमं सदा।
संबंधसप्रतिभुवं धनं दद्याच्च साक्षिमत्।।
गृहीत लिखितं योग्यमानं प्रत्यागमे सुखम्।
न दद्याद् वृद्धिलोभेन नष्टं मूलधनं भवेत्।।
आहारे व्यवहारे च त्यक्त लज्जः सुखी भवेत्।
धनं मैत्रीकरं दाने चोदाने शत्रुकारकम्।।
(Driştvādharmanam vrīdhyāpi vyavahāraksḿ sadā
Sambandhasapratibhuvaḿ dhanaḿ dadyācca sākşimat
Grihīta likhitam yogyamānaḿ pratyāgame sukhaḿ
Na dadyād vrīdhilobhen naştaḿ mūldhanam bhavet
Āhāre vyavhāre ca tyakta lajjah sukhi bhavet
Dhanaḿ maitrikaraḿ dāne codāne śtrukārkam)

— *Śukra Nitih (3-192, 193, 194)*

On the basis of the capacity of the borrower to pay interest, the loan may be given on the basis of mortgage deed or surety bond furnished by another person. Such deed or bond must be written along with the witnesses. The amount of loan should be only such a reasonable amount of money that can be paid back easily and comfortably. Any other method must not be adopted for the greed of earning interest because in that event, even the loss of the principal amount cannot be ruled out. In the matters of trade or business, the terms of lending and borrowing must be sufficiently clear. It should be considered that the money lent creates friendship but turns into enmity at the time of its repayment by the borrower to the lender.

All the conditions prescribed in the matter of lending money are based on one main condition that lack of frankness and ambiguity in terms and conditions are likely to place even the principal amount in jeopardy and ultimately results in spoiling mutual relationship.

Another point of wisdom is that only that amount ought to be lent that the other person may be capable of being returned along with interest with ease. If heavy amount of money is lent, the repayment of which and the interest thereon becomes difficult, the borrower tries to evade the lender as far as possible. The borrower takes no time in forgetting the help rendered by the lender and starts cursing him. This is the usual case, exceptions apart. The series of wisdom prescribed by Śukra are quite relevant even in thc modern times, though presented thousands of years back in time.

Loan to a Friend

Though, it has been said that money lending may lead to enmity, yet it has been suggested by Śukra, that on asking, a friend may be given a loan without interest. The advice goes to the extent that even if the earlier loan may not have been paid back, there is no harm in allowing further debt. No doubt, the charging of interest alone has been relaxed for friends but not the other conditions. Śukra clarifies that the debt with or without interest to a friend should not be given unless a loan deed has been written and signed by the parties and the witnesses.

Economic and Social Justice

A special feature regarding the extent of interest payment is:

यदा चतुर्गुणा वृद्धिर्गृहीता धनिकेन च।
अधमर्णान्न दातव्यं धनिने तु धनं तदा।।
(Yadā caturgunā vriḍhirgrịhītā dhaniken ca
Adhmrnānna dātavyaḿ dhanine to dhanantadā)

— *Śukra Nitih (3-203, 204)*

When, interest amount paid equals to four times the principal debt, then the debt should be considered as fully paid and nothing more should be paid to the moneylender.

This is a singular example of economic and social justice prevailing in the ancient period, which has not yet seen a reality in the modern times. Our leaders have been talking and preaching about such pieces of justice but the reality has been different.

Protection of Wealth

Protection, which includes preservation as well as growth, had been one of the considerations even during the Vedic period. Advising the Prajapati, it has been said:

> उपोहश्च समूहश्च क्षत्तारौ ते प्रजापते।
> ताविहा वहतां स्फाति बहु भूमान मक्षितम्।।
> (Upohśca camukahśca kṣttārau te prājapate,
> Tāvihā vahatāṁ sphāti bahu bhumān maksitaṁ)
>
> — *Atharva Veda (3-24-7)*

O! Prajapati, those who earn wealth as well as those who preserve and protect, both are the treasures. They may bring enormous wealth here and may preserve and protect the same.

Here also the emphasis is on preservation and protection of wealth. Śukra has laid down a novel method of preservation and protection of wealth. He says:

> यथा न जानान्तिं धनं संचितं कतिकुत्र वै।
> आत्मस्त्री पुत्र मित्राणि सलेखं धारयेत्तथा।।
> (Yathā na jānāntim dhanam sancitaṁ katikutra vai
> ātmastri putra mitrāni salekhaṁ dhāryettathā)
>
> — *Śukra Nitih (3-188)*

One should try that his wife, son or friends too may not know how much money is kept and where. Aimed at its growth, one may lend it on interest after proper writing of deeds, but should not keep the money at home for the reason that it may be difficult to protect it if the wife and sons know about of it. Śukra, being the teacher of demons, had full knowledge of the working of evil. He had conceptualised the way to check the evil. He, therefore, warned the people that the extent of the wealth should be kept a secret. The one who may not be inclined to accept the authenticity of the advice is free to give it a try. Many share the views related to the secrecy about how much wealth is kept where besides, the allied idea is that the money may be given as debt. This helps the growth of money in two ways. In the first place, the principal amount swells with the addition of the interest. Some friend or needy person, facing financial crisis may be helped, if the money remains safe and protected and its misuse is avoided.

Public Borrowing

Modern money management also has the practice of public borrowing by the state. This practice becomes more relevant in the context of the state being in business, controlling mammoth industrial organisations. On this issue, it has been said:

> धनिकेभ्यो भृतिं दत्वा स्वापत्तौ तद्धनं हरेत।
> राजा स्वापत्समुत्तीर्णतत स्वं दद्यात सवृद्धिकम।।
> (Dhanikebhya bhritim datva svapattau taddhanam haret
> Raja svapatsamuttirntat svam daddyat savridhiam)
>
> — *Śukra Nitih (3-198)*
>
> *When faced with calamities, the King (state) may borrow from the rich persons on the promise of paying interest. When calamities are over, the money borrowed should be returned with interest.*

Such practice of public borrowing has many advantages. Patriotism and commitment towards the state are developed. The state generates its own resources of wealth. The accumulated and idle money gets protected and gainfully utilised. Thus, there is nothing new in the concept of public borrowing by the state. In India, this was being practised long back during ancient period.

Advice for All

There is a piece of advice for one and all in the context of money management.

> सदारप्रौढपुत्रान् द्राक श्रेयोऽर्थी विभजेत पिता।
> सदारभ्रातरः प्रौढा विभजेयुः परस्परम्।
> (Sadār praudhaputrān drāk shreyorthi vibhjet pitā
> Sadār bhrātaraḥ prauḍha vibhajeyuh parasparam)
>
> — *Śukra Nitih*
>
> *The one who seeks his own welfare should distribute the wealth amongst his married and employed sons, so that there may not arise any dispute over property in future. In the same way, even*

real brothers after getting married and employed should divide the property. If that is not done, they are likely to harm themselves in the course of quarrels and litigations etc.

This advice has many hidden advantages, though may appear to be division-oriented. The main advantage is that when the father divides the property in his lifetime, the one aggrieved has the chance of approaching the father and request for a review. The other advantage is that the father also gets a chance to see how his property is getting utilised. Another big advantage is that all the matters become so clear that there hardly remains any scope for disputes in the future.

The foregoing thoughts about money management present only a glimpse that the Indian thinkers had the wisdom to conceive such intricate ideas in this area. The enlightened readers may take a cue from such thoughts.

OO

15

On Saying 'No'

The Forms of 'No'

Saying 'no' assumes various forms. A terse expression, in parliamentary language, in injunctive style, showing disagreement with some view, rejecting a favour sought, refusing to give away something and a host of other ways. Each one is expressed with a difference.

Parliamentary 'No'

An issue raised as a question in an Assembly or Parliament is to be negated. There are two mainly possible ways. One may be 'No, sir'. As against this terse 'no', the reply could be, "The question is answered in negative". Both of these expressions convey the same meaning; yet, one is just a crude reply and the other is couched in parliamentary language. The former may hurt, while the later may not.

Injunctive 'No'

The injunctive style may be seen in scriptures of all faiths. Indian scriptures, generally, contain the injunctions of directions and prohibitions. For example:

> युद्धकृयां विना सैन्यं योजयेन्नान्यकर्मणि ।
> (Yuddhkṛyāṁ vinā sainyaṁ yojyennānya karmani)
>
> — *Śukra Nitih (5-93)*
>
> *Army should not be used for any other purpose other than those connected with battles, wars and defence of nation. (Direction containing negation)*

विभज्य दण्डः कर्तव्यो धर्मेण न यदृच्छया।

(Vibhajya dandaḥ kartavyo dharmen na yadṛcchaya)

— *Mahabharata Shanti Parva (122-40)*

Punishment should be awarded as per rules and after careful consideration. Punishment should not be based on whims and caprices. (Direction containing prohibition)

Disagreement with Views

Negative reply is also given if one does not agree with some view presented. In this situation, one may have to say, "No, I do not agree." Such reply may be taken as unpleasant. The reply may be given as, "I do not agree, my view is so and so for such and such reasons." This style has widely been used by Kautilya in his *Aratha Śastra*. Deliberating upon the views of other thinkers that, if the employer does not give work when the worker has presented himself for the work, the work shall be considered as done, Kautilya says:

नेति कौटिल्यः कृतस्य वेतनं नाकृतस्यास्ति।

(Neti Kautilyaḥ, kṛtasya vetanaṁ nākṛtasyāsti)

— *Artha Śastra (3-14-7, 8)*

'No' says Kautilya. A wage is for the work done, not for what is not done.

Commenting upon the view of the thinkers in general, Kautilya shows his disagreement, but that is not all. If he had only said '*Neti Kautilyah*', it might have been taken as a terse 'no'. But Kautilya chose to go further and give his views supported by reasons.

Refusal of Favours or Things

Then come up for consideration the remaining two ways of saying 'no' — rejecting a favour sought and refusing to give away something. In these situations again, the reply could be a terse 'no' or some other way which may not hurt the one who faces the refusal. In such situations, saying 'no' is an art which is rare. In the matter of rejecting a favour sought, situations arise in which promises are either forgotten or not fulfilled.

Promises Not Fulfilled

There is a famous proverb, "Promises easily made are difficult to keep". This generally is the case of the promises, which are forgotten. Most people make easy promises, may be to gain cheap popularity or just to show off or to get rid of the one seeking favour.

However, if one knows the value of making promises and the obligations arising out of them, he will make only well-considered promises. Fulfilling the promises made is one of the highest human values. This was the cherished characteristic of Sri Ram, the picture of an ideal Indian man.

In the context of fulfilling the promise made, Śukra said:

करिष्यामिति ते कार्यं न कुर्यात्कार्यलम्बनम् ।
द्राक्कुर्यात्त समर्थश्चेत्साशं दीर्घं न रक्षयेत् । ।
(Karişya miti te karyaṁ na kuryatkaryalambanam
Drakkuryatta samarthścetsaśaṁ dirghaṁ na rakşyet)

— *Śukra Nitih (2-232)*

After promising someone that "I shall do your work", one should not keep it pending. If the person making the promise is competent, he should do it himself or he should get it done. One should not be kept waiting for long.

Not keeping the promises is a double-edged sword that cuts both ways. It causes pain hurts and demoralises the person to whom the promise is made. At the same time, it damages the image, personality and reputation of the person making false promises. He loses his credibility and is ridiculed.

The quality of fulfilling the promises made helps in maintaining cordial human relations. Keeping someone waiting is agonising. The person promised might develop ill will for the one who makes such promises. People lose faith in such person. In the process, irreparable harm is caused not only to the person concerned but also to the whole value system of the society. A manager behaving in such manner tends to lose his personal power.

Hope Causes Agony

A promise creates hope, which if not fulfilled causes stress and strain and is thus painful. Relevant to this thought, the *Mahabharata* has said:

आशा हि बलवती राजन नैराश्यं परमं सुखम्।
(Āśā hi balavati Rājan nairāsyaṁ paramaṁsukham)

— Mahabharata Shanti Parva (178-8-1)

Hope is so powerful that it causes pain; losing hope is comfortable and pleasing.

A hopeful person lives under a tiring stress, always expecting the fulfilment of hope. Such constant waiting causes agony. However, if there remains no hope, there is no waiting; one lives in peace — free from tension. Yet in the state of hopelessness the hope sometimes gets fulfilled, which gives more pleasure than otherwise.

Saying 'Yes'

A general feeling is that saying 'no' is unpleasant, blunt and hurtful. But this is not a well-founded view. Even pleasant messages can be given in an unpleasant manner and the 'painful no' can be conveyed in pleasing manner. The only difference lies in the skill of expression.

As against the dexterity of saying 'no', there are people, who as a part of their habit, say 'yes'. But this too is not simple. Just like saying 'no', saying 'yes' is also an art. Here is an example of a renounced advocate of Allahabad High Court.

Mr. Girdhari Lal, a seasoned advocate, firmly adhered to the rule of always saying 'yes'. He was, once arguing a second appeal, involving an intricate point of law. The judge was not agreeing with his submissions, but Mr. Girdhari Lal went on pressing his point so much that the judge exhausted his patience and with annoyance, remarked, "Mr. Agrawal, do you consider me a fool?" "Yes, my lord!" came the prompt reply. Mr. Girdhari Lal, however, immediately realised the abnormality of the offence and apologised.

The people known as 'yes man' have since increased and a new creed is growing in number. Such people make high promises easily and with the same ease forget them.

Saying 'No'

Wisdom lies in appreciation and understanding of a situation when to say 'yes' and when 'no'. Credibility of a person is established by the number of 'yes' coming true and also by honesty in saying 'no'. A person who knows how to say 'no' is known for his straightforwardness.

Saying 'no' is in itself an art, a skill. A bluntly said 'no' is liable to cause pain to the one who is replied thus. At times, it may also cause verbal injury.

A negative message deserves to be conveyed in a way that its recipient does not get hurt; otherwise it is better to say nothing but just to keep quiet. The relevant saying is:

"Na bruyat satyam apriyam"

Do not speak the unpleasant truth.

Example of Saying 'No'

A large number of examples of offending 'no' and also the sophisticated ones are available in *Mahabharata*, the great epic.

Krishna as emissary of the Pandavas went to the kingdom of Kauravas at Hastinapur. With all efforts having failed, he ultimately asked for only five villages for the Pandavas, only to avoid the battle and the bloodshed. But Duryodhana, bluntly said that he would not give even an inch of earth without armed confrontation. This was an example of a rude 'no'. So Krishna came back, disappointed. It was settled that there would be a decisive battle.

The two sides, Pandavas and Kaurvas, therefore started preparations. They sought help from various kings and chieftains. Duryodhana was well aware that Krishna was the well-wisher of Pandavas, yet, he went to solicit his help. Now Krishna could have also replied in the same manner by saying 'no' rudely, but his culture and personality would not resort to such crude method. Instead, he offered his well-equipped army for one side and he himself alone and unarmed for the other. Since he saw Arjuna first, so he had the first choice. Arjuna opted for Krishna unarmed. Not understanding Arjuna's wisdom, Duryodhana was overjoyed to get the well-equipped army of Krishna for his side.

Krishna did not want to say 'no' to Duryodhana for his own help, so knowing the wisdom that Arjuna possessed, he made the deft offer. Such is the wisdom of saying 'no'. Krishna's style of negative reply was not at all hurting, though he had denied the greatest asset to Duryodhana.

Mother's 'No'

Mother in every household is faced with the problems. Children keep making demands for many things. Many a times some demands are impossible to fulfil. For example, a child wants to have the moon. If the mother says 'no', the young one may start crying. So the mother, instead of saying 'no', shows moon's image in water which is near at hand and thus satisfies the impossible demand. The mothers all over, devise their own means of saying 'no' to many demands of the children. Many a times, on one pretext or the other, they sidetrack the demand, which is forgotten after some time. On occasions, mother puts her own conditions. In the process, she gets many errands performed, gets homework done or gets the children rid of some bad habit. Mother usually does not say 'no' as she knows the art.

Mahabharata Views

Denying some favour or to give something, if not done wisely, may go to the extent of causing verbal injury, which is worse than bodily injury. A wound may get healed up in due course of time but a verbal injury may not. *Mahabharata* cautions in this context by saying:

वाचा दुरुक्तं बीभत्सम न संरोहति वाक्क्षतम् ।

(Vacaā duruktamí bībhatsam na sanrohāti vakkṣtam)

Mahabharata Udyog Parva (34-78)

The wounds caused by hurting words are so fierce that they do not get healed up.

It is true that the hurting words make their own place in the mind and get erupted at appropriate moments. 'No' is also one such hurting word, if not used with caution. If some request is bluntly denied, the negative message remains activated for very long and comes out with violent flames when suited atmosphere is available. It is, therefore, appropriate and proper to exercise full caution in saying 'no'.

Relevance to Industry

The skill of saying 'yes' or 'no' is of relevance for the managers — the captains of industry. Manager has to perform a variety of functions in relation to the workforce. His 'yes' or 'no' must appear of some worth. For example, take workers' demands related to their problems.

A large number of demands are usually placed before the managers. Some of these can be easily accepted but some cannot be by any means. The manager should, for the first type of demands say 'yes', but not in a way that the workers do not perceive any worth of it. The 'yes' should also appear to be valuable. If such strategy is adopted wisely, the sharpness of the difficult and impossible demands can be made blunt. Now, taking the demands, which cannot be granted, there is one way that the manger may refuse by a rough 'no', but at what cost? Agitation may sprout up and create a difficult situation. Alternatively, the wise manager may adopt an approach, which may not be harsh or rough. One such tactic is not to discuss such demands, which can be accepted and negotiations may proceed on the difficult ones. If the negotiations go ahead on easy and pleasant note, the sharp edge of the difficult ones may get blunt. Another possibility is that the workers may get weary and may look forward for getting some demands accepted. If the acceptable demands are thus met, the workers may get satisfied and the difficult ones might get sidetracked. In the process, both 'yes' and 'no' may become valuable.

The skill of saying 'yes' or 'no' can be used in different situations, for instance, in matters of discipline, industrial relations, interpersonal relation and so on. Yet it may not be possible to evolve any universally applicable formula to cater to the needs of all. Managers will have to depend largely on their prudence, the situation, the environment, the approach, the relative strength of the parties, backing and support available to them and so on. They will have to develop their own strategies in view of the variables as stated here.

Negation of Grievance

Saying 'no' calls for a greater wisdom in yet another area of industrial relations — the grievance handling. A grievance that can be resolved must be cleared quickly. This will strengthen the effectiveness of the manager. If one worker's grievance is resolved by the manager, the message spreads all over. The manager's personal power increases and he becomes more effective. However, if the grievance cannot be resolved at the manager's level, he must write to the competent authority giving his recommendations. Yet, if it cannot be met, the worker ought to be informed along with the reasons for the negative decision. If the worker gets this sort of reply, he tends to be satisfied as he knows the reasons and can proceed further if he so desires. He has the satisfaction that the matter has at least been properly considered. The negative reply in such a case is not painful or hurting.

Conclusion

The essence of saying 'no' is very simple and also a skill for those who care for the interpersonal relations. The artless art of saying 'no' is being practised and experienced since long in the remote past and various new ways and means have been developed in the process. It is an essential skill not only for the managers but also for all men, women and children who interact with others. It is an important human value, which carries people towards perfection.

OO

16

On Contradicting

Contradiction Unfolded

Agreeing with some view is simple and so is disagreeing. Contradicting is a shade more serious than disagreeing. To contradict is understood as, to oppose by words, to speak against, to deny what is affirmed or to assert the contrary. It is in this view that contradicting someone usually tends to cause annoyance. It is, therefore, taken as a barrier to effective relationship.

It is quite usual that one may not agree with the views of another. In that case, one may keep quiet, may politely show his disagreement giving the reasons or may contradict.

The people who contradict can usually be divided into three broad categories — those who bluntly contradict a view, those who contradict with all niceties and sophistication, and yet others who say nothing but contradict by deeds and actions. These contradicting people are usually in 'I am right, you are not right' or 'critical parent ego' state of the personality.

Though, the contradicting people are not able to maintain amicable interpersonal relationship; yet, the wise amongst them, deftly camouflage their contradiction to the extent that the one contradicted takes it easy, the question of getting hurt may hardly arise. Otherwise, generally the contradictions cause annoyance and may even cause verbal injury.

Sukra's View

Mainly because of the serious consequences that contradicting has been decried by Śukra even in joking situations thus:

> सुखप्रबन्धगोष्ठीषु विवादे वादिनां मतम् ।
> विजानन्नपि नो ब्रूयाम्दर्तुः क्षिपत्वोत्तरं वचः ।।
>
> (Sukhaprabandh goṣthīṣu vivāde vādinaṁ matam,
> Vijānannāpi no brūyādbhartuḥ kṣptavottraṁ vacaḥ)
>
> — *Śukra Nitih*
>
> *In the sittings organised for entertainment purposes, in the event of any difference of opinion arising during discussions, if the King expresses a view, the wise one should not contradict even if seized of the principles involved.*

That being the demand of wisdom, those who want to be effective and successful ought to adopt a policy of either being at a bay from contradictions or to manage the situation deftly. Instead of diverting from the goal only to satisfy the ego, one should avoid contradictions and take a realistic and practical view of things.

A Relevant Example

Taking an example, once the Emperor Akbar in his *darbar* said to Birbal:

Akbar : See Birbal, what a nice vegetable brinjal is!

Birbal : Your majesty! That is why it has a crown on its head.

The emperor appreciated Birbal's ready wit. After a few days, the emperor again remarked:

Akbar: Brinjal is a nasty and useless vegetable.

Birbal: Your majesty! That is why it is named 'be-gun' (worthless).

Soon thereafter, Faizy, another courtier said:

Faizy: Birbal! The other day you praised brinjal when his majesty appreciated it. You said that it had a crown on its head, but now when his majesty talked ill of it, you are saying that the brinjal is bad and only for that reason it is named 'be-gun'.

Now all eyes turned toward Birbal, who promptly replied:

Birbal: This humble being serves his majesty and not the brinjal.

Thus, Birbal not only acted on the wisdom prescribed by Śukra as aforesaid, but also aimed towards his goal that a courtier must express his views wisely without causing annoyance to the boss. In fact, Birbal had expressed both possible views and yet did not displease the emperor.

The Proper Moment

No effort is being made to suggest that one should become a total 'yes man'. But the fact remains that it is also no wisdom to become a 'no man'. Śukra has suggested that a wise man even seized of the principles should not contradict the boss. If one, on the basis of the knowledge desists from contradiction in view of the demand of time and situation and keeps quiet, that is a practical way. Any untimely utterance may lead to serious consequences. Realising the appropriateness of time and situation, if a wise person can avoid confrontation at one time, he will surely get an opportune moment to put forth his view based on the principles. It is all a matter of timing the replies properly.

One ought to consider why people contradict. It may be because they do not wish to deviate from their principles, they want to put forth their view come what may, they want to fan their ego, or they feel that what they feel is the only correct idea and so on. Yet there appears no reason why rigidity may be allowed a free play. A workable practical method may easily be adopted.

The Two Replies

Under no circumstances, contradiction should be allowed to cause verbal injury. An example may clarify the position.

A *talluqa* case was being heard for several days in the Chief Court of Awadh by Justice Sir Wazir Hasan. Sir Tej Bahadur Sapru was appearing for one of the parties. On the fourth day Sir Wazir Hasan jocularly remarked, "It is very unfair, Sir Tej. You are getting Rs 3000/- per day, while I am getting only Rs 100/- for dealing with this very case." Sir Tej promptly replied, "My lord, it is only a difference of three feet or so. You have just to cross the bar and earn Rs 3000/- a day." Sir Wazir naturally felt complimented.

A few months later, in another *talluqa* case, Mr. Mohammad Ali Jinnah appeared before Sir Wazir Hasan. This case also continued for several days. On the third day of the arguments, Sir Wazir repeated the same to Mr. Jinnah saying that he was getting Rs 3000/- a day while he, the judge, got only Rs 100/- per day. Mr. Jinnah at once replied, "My lord, it may appear to be unfortunate but everybody is paid according to his capacity." This deeply hurt Sir Wazir Hasan and he did not repeat the said remark to any other counsel in future.

The difference between the two repartees is visible, one compliments while the other causes serious verbal injury. In both the cases, the judge's version was contradicted; one created goodwill and the other was painful to the extent that the judge was totally stunned and never could dare to ask the same question even jocularly.

The Other Pattern

Once being cross-examined by Pandit Moti Lal Nehru, a senior military officer, in spite of being warned by the court, continued to object to the question on the ground that they were irrelevant or unnecessary. The military officer finally said to Pandit Moti Lal Nehru, "Do you think me to be a fool?" Pandit Nehru promptly replied, "Of course not!" and then quietly added, "But I may be mistaken". This example has a bright blending of contradiction and non-contradiction both, but in such a subtle way that everyone laughed it away and no injury was caused.

There is yet another example of an open contradiction. Sir Tej's house was the rendezvous of the leading men of the town, as well as of numerous visitors from outside. Once, a friend's son, fresh from Oxford came to see Sir Tej. Finding an atmosphere of extreme politeness, the young man said, "Babuji, I find there is overflowing politeness here, which looks so feudal. Instead of expression, there is too much of *takalluf* (formality). For example, '*Aiye! Tashrif laiye*' (come please, your gracious self) etc." Sir Tej jocularly remarked, "Yes, my dear young man! I think when you came I should have said, '*abe aa baith ja*' (come, sirra, sit down)."

These are just a few examples about contradictions coming from the elite. Several others can be seen from different classes of society. Though generalisations cannot be drawn, the fact remains that the tact must be used in situations of contradiction. Tact, in simple expressions, is the art of recognising when to be big and not to be little. It is a knack of making a point without making an enemy.

Contradiction by Acts

Contradiction is not by words alone. There are contradictions by deeds and actions as well. Many such actions can come within the scope of misconduct. Yet, a large number of actions are such that they constitute contradiction, but are taken as acts of humility and courtesy. For example, an assistant visiting the chamber of a very senior officer do not take seat even when the officer asks him to sit, in the name of humility. There are some officers who take note of such action. The assistant is again offered a seat but he politely says 'I am alright, sir'. They ultimately sit only when the officer gets annoyed. This is a case of contradicting by action.

A person was supervising the works out in the open sun in the summer month of May. His father, on this sight, politely asked him to take the umbrella, which the servant carried for him. But he neither went to a shady corner nor took the umbrella. The father, a wise person, then called the servant and asked him to take the little grandson and play with him in the open heat of the sun. That was done; now seeing his little one in the sun, he shouted at the servant and ordered him to take him in shade. The father promptly said to his grownup son that his heart also beats for the safety of his son. On this, the young man smilingly took umbrella and got a shade over his head. Such examples are many, but often go unnoticed and unthought-of. The acts of contradiction thus go on and on.

A Positive Stand

In an interpersonal relationship, it is of prime importance that while making a point one should not offend the other person in any way. Such action may lead to serious consequences. The spoken words have to be so chosen that views may get expressed and the other may not feel that the person is treating him as inferior. One ought to come from 'I am right, you are not right' to 'I am right, you are also right', that is, the adult ego state. One should consider that others too are knowledgeable and are speaking on some basis. If one has a different view, he must present it in a way so as to become acceptable; otherwise, the view will be rejected and the attitude may cause annoyance to others.

Conclusion

Therefore, taking all precautions, using tact and applying wisdom, the safer course of action is to adopt a practical policy of least resistance. But the chances can also not be ruled out that practising so one may tend to become a soft-spoken person, which in turn may cause some problems. It may, therefore, be appropriate to keep in view an advice from Śukra, which says:

मार्दवान्नेव गणयेदपमानोऽतिवादतः ।

(Mārdvānneva ganayedapamānoati vādataḥ)

— *Śukra Nitih (3-220)*

A soft-spoken or extremely polite person is not cared for. A person, who speaks much, too faces humiliation often.

However, another view relevant to this situation is available in *Mahabharata*, which says:

नासाध्यं मृदुना किंचित ।

(Nāsādhyaṁ mṛduna kincit)

— *Mahabharata Vana Parva (28-37)*

There is nothing which soft-spoken person cannot achieve.

This view gives a different picture of a soft-spoken person. Both the views are correct according to the person, the situation, the occasion and the setting, etc. A wise person ought to keep both in the action plan; preferably a nice blending of both.

Therefore, the golden rule that emerges is to adopt a middle path. Our actions should be goal-oriented. One must adopt a strategy of contradicting or not contradicting, keeping in view the goal achievement. It is better if one cultivates the habit of not contradicting. However, if contradicting may be necessary one must take a decision that if the goal achievement is pushed back by contradicting, it may not be wise to be resorted to. Another wisdom that gets attracted is that contradiction may not be so sharp-edged as to cause verbal injury to others. Contradictions resorted to with skill may not hamper effective interpersonal relationship and may also promote goodwill and amity amongst people. All that is needed is a thoughtful and goal-oriented action plan.

○○

Epilogue

This book on managerial prudence now comes to a transient close in the sense that at some later stage, more and more thoughts may solicit their inclusion in it. However, the book needs the attention of the class of erudite readers to check for the errors and omissions which might have inadvertently crept in. It is for such reason that conclusions of the chapters are mostly open-ended. The study is open and continuing.

Management thinkers and scholars have constantly been propounding their latest theories. In the modern period, significant contributions have been made by the thinkers of Europe and America. These experts have made considerable contributions. From Robert Owen (1771-1858), who is known as 'the first manager' to Peter F. Drucker, the most influential living management thinker, various scholars in the field have given new concepts to the science of management. This study would remain incomplete without the mention of F.W. Taylor, who is widely known as 'Father of Scientific Management'.

In India, various experiments have either been tried or are in the process. On the thought side, no significant contribution appears to be in sight. Nevertheless, our past has been glorious. The Indian scriptures, like *Mahabharata*, *Srimad Bhagvat Gita*, *Artha Śastra*, *Śukra Nitih*, *Manu Smriti*, *Nārad Nitih*, *Valmiki Ramayana*, and all the Vedas and Upanishads are a vast reservoir of wisdom on management. Efforts have been made to present only a glimpse of all that in this work; much is yet to follow in due course. The sole purpose is to attract more and more thinkers in this field to explore intensively.

The material, directly or indirectly connected with management has been classified into chapters, described and briefly commented upon. Not that this is a pioneering work, many scholars have made considerable contributions on different scriptures. The effort in this work has been to combine the prudence from different scriptures at one place.

The fact remains that the modern foreign experts have evolved their theories of which Indian scriptures have been the forerunners.

Based on the knowledge contained in the scriptures, Indian managements do not need experiments. Indian thought can justly be called the seed of the management. India is the fittest and the most conducive place for the success of these ideas. What the foreign thinkers have said is a part of all that is contained in the Indian scriptures.

Robert Owen emphasised that management ought to win the confidence of workers, should educate and develop them. Similar ideas have been discussed by Śukra in *Śukra Nitih* and Kautilya in *Artha Śastra*, references to which can be found in the chapters 'Cultivate Your Workforce' and 'Discipline'. Owen's idea was that punishment need not be used as a means of discipline and that man be moulded by education and environment. So the worker needs to be taught to be disciplined. Such ideas with wider scope can be seen in the chapter 'Discipline'. Most of the ideas contained in Owen's book *A New View of Society* can be seen based on Indian scriptures.

George Elton Mayo's research, 'Hawthorne Experiments' (1927-1933), precisely led to the conclusion that workers can go to the heights of performance, if accorded proper recognition and appreciation. Indian scriptures are full of such ideas and few examples can be seen in *ślokas* in the chapter 'The Basic Managerial Functions'.

Mary Parker Fallatt's philosophy has been called 'Dynamic Philosophy of Management'. But the total message from the scriptures is much more dynamic in nature. Her views were that life would be dull, if there are no conflicts, therefore it would be wise to make it creative, the same way we create music from violin. This view can be seen in the chapter 'Crisis Management'.

Henri Fayol was the General Manager of a big coal and metallurgical concern in France. He was mostly attentive to the problems of top management. He developed 'The Theory of Principles of Administration'. He believed that 'to govern is to foresee'. His faith was 'discipline is what managers make it'. If they are disciplined the entire organisation becomes so. His watchword was 'preach by example'. Glimpses of such views in Indian scriptures may be seen in the chapter titled 'Management by Example'. Most of Fayol's other views can also be seen in varied contexts.

Oliver Sheldon of Great Britain has mainly dealt with the social responsibilities of management in his book, *The Philosophy of Management*. This aspect has been vividly taken up in the injunctions in the scriptures. Besides, most of his other thoughts find place in the chapter 'The Regulatory Provisions'. Similar are the thoughts of S. Rowntree of Great Britain.

Human dignity is one aspect that has been emphasised by most thinkers, like Oliver Sheldon, Moslow, McGregor, Drucker, Chris Argyris, and finds a prominent place in the 'IBM Philosophy'. This dignity factor occupies a prominent place in most of the Indian scriptures, *Śukra Nitih* in particular.

Leadership has been discussed by many thinkers, like Chris Argyris, Rensis Likert, and many others. Most of them have enumerated leadership traits; Likert has conceived manager as a leader. However, leadership is the subject matter of the chapter entitled 'Manager as Leader', which is based on Indian scriptures.

Douglas McGregor has propounded the thoughts on developing and training managers. Besides, training of personnel has been richly contributed by David McChalland, who has said that training of personnel aims at developing achievement motivation. IBM has developed a philosophy of training as a continuous process. Amongst Indian scholars, Kautilya has contributed in this area, the obvious reason being that he was basically a teacher of the people. A teacher can best appreciate the need of training and also differentiate between teaching and training. While the chapter 'Self Development' deals with development of management executives; the references from *Artha Śastra* regarding the training of personnel is available in the chapter 'Training'.

Peter F. Drucker has professed his thoughts on time management as time is a very precious resource in the hands of managers. However, this aspect has received the desired attention of ancient Indian thinkers. A very brief view may be had from a few *ślokas* of the chapter 'The Basic Managerial Functions' and at other places as well, which the enlightened readers will easily identify.

Rensis Likert has said that managements should listen to workforce, have trust in them and accept their suggestions. All such wise acts have been deliberated upon by Indian thinkers in the remote.

Collective bargaining has been deliberated upon by many modern thinkers, like Douglas McGregor and Allan Flanders. In their view, it increases cooperation, efficiency and leads to prosperity. On the Indian scene, Kautilya, in his *Artha Śastra*, has dealt with this subject.

There are some chapters in which I have not made any comparison, but have talked only of the principles elaborated in the ancient scriptures and also creative literature. The chapter dealing with the crisis management is one such example. I have given this chapter the sub-title as 'Hanuman — The Great Crisis Manager'. I hope you would like to know why I have called this legendary hero, the crisis manager. Tulsidas, the great poet of medieval India, has written a long poem in the honour of Hanuman, with very deep religious sentiments, calling him '*sankat mochan*'. This adjective gave me the idea that I should try to analyse Hanuman's personality and also his life, as a good crisis manager. A crisis manager is virtually a translation of the word combination '*sankat mochan*'. The character and personality of Hanuman as an excellent manager of the crisis was first developed by the great Indian poet Valmiki in his *Ramayana*. In this great epic poem, we find Hanuman managing one crisis after the other with the help of his disciplined speech, intelligent behaviour, competent handling of intricate situations, valour and many other attributes. The managers going through this chapter will learn how to face the crisis and resolve it, of course, with full confidence.

Hanuman's role as a crisis manager has also been explored in the chapter 'Manage Your Speaking'. Speaking has been defined as the goal-oriented messages between the people to meet the target needs. Speaking has been said to be like waging a war in which no one succeeds, if he does not plan or organise the strategy beforehand. This pre-planning is necessary not only for what to say, but also for how to say it. Our sages are of the opinion that in order to say something properly, one ought to know the proper use of the language, as a means for communication. A manager spends more of his time in communication than in other activities; therefore it is absolutely necessary for him to have a good command over language.

The great thinkers of India have said that the first essential for good speaking or the proper use of language is '*vak sanyam*'. They fully realised that the complete '*vak sanyam*', that is, the full control of speech is not possible, but they also accept that if we do not discipline our speech, we will be inviting trouble. Therefore, it is absolutely essential that one should constantly remain alert in controlling his tongue. A manager continuously remains engaged in communication, sometimes through verbal media and at other occasions in writing with his fellow officers and other co-workers. Therefore, it is even more necessary for him that he should understand and also practise the proper use of language. A slip of tongue or a wrong word in writing may create havoc. Our sages have, therefore, written much about the art of speaking. Let me summarise what the scriptures have said to avoid undesirable situations.

Our great thinkers have advised that one should speak only at the proper time and also on the right occasion. He should speak the truth and nothing but the truth. But this truth should be spoken only if it is pleasant and also beneficial not only for the person who is being addressed but also for the humanity at large. However, this should also be kept in mind that whatever is being said should not in any way hurt the dignity of the person with whom he is talking. One should never speak on the spur of the moment; every word should come out from the mouth after deep thinking, while trying to learn how to be a good speaker, one should also try to be a good listener. He should also try to understand the problem with the person with whom he is speaking and then alone he should open his mouth. While speaking, one should also know when to stop. I have found Hanuman an ideal speaker and I sincerely hope that one who goes through his life, an analysis of which I have presented, will learn much from him and succeed in any branch of life he may be.

A manager has not only to speak but he also has to convey his ideas, intentions and messages in writing. The sages have also offered very many suggestions for proper writing. They have regarded writing as a skill which can be acquired and developed by continuous practice. Guru Śukra writes that a good writer should be proficient in calculation, conversant with the variations of the language, doubtless and capable of conveying the ideas clearly and logically. The great politician Kautilya has further elaborated the ideas about the successful writing. He has classified the written matters into thirteen categories, mentioned seven types of documents, five kinds of deficiencies in writing and six attributes for being a good writer. All these have been covered in the chapter 'Manage Your Writing'. The ideas presented by Kautilya will be useful not only for gaining managerial excellence, but for anyone who wants to convey his ideas through his pen.

The ancient scriptures are replete with highly developed principles for other fields of management as well, such as discipline, regulatory provisions for industrial establishments, money management, training of personnel and other connected matters. In the end, I have also added two chapters, 'On Saying No' and 'On Contradicting'. In these chapters, I have strictly confined myself to the matter available in the ancient Indian scriptures. All this material clearly shows how our sages had observed the different aspects of life. I sincerely hope that this study inspires the scholars of deeper understanding and abilities to explore the vast ocean of the ancient Indian scriptures and literature further.

ᴐᴐ